WHY I CEASED TO BE A REVOLUTIONARY

BEGINNINGS + ENDS

WHY I CEASED TO BE A REVOLUTIONARY

BEGINNINGS + ENDS

LEV TIKHOMIROV

Translated by K. Benois

TAXIARCH PRESS
2020

Why I Ceased to Be a Revolutionary
Published in Russian as *Почему я перестал быть
революционером*
Published by Nouvelle Librairie Parisienne, Paris 1888

Beginnings and Ends
Published in Russian as *Начала и концы*
Published by University Press, Moscow 1890

English Translation
©Taxiarch Press 2020
©K. Benois 2020
Printed by Amazon KDP 2020
All rights reserved
Zvolen, Slovakia/London, England

Any and all queries
we ask you to email us at taxiarch.press@yandex.com
We can be followed on Twitter at @TaxiarchPress

ISBN: **9798692774606**

Cover design by Andrej Sennoy

Lev Tikhomirov in the 1890s

Lev Tikhomirov as a student radical

Contents

About the Author

Lev Alexandrovich Tikhomirov was born on January 19th, 1852, in Gelendzhik, a Russian town not far from the Kerch strait. While his father, a successful military doctor, worked at the town's fort, he was brought up by his mother, a pious woman prone to episodes of religious hysteria. His childhood unfolded during a critical time for Russia. Born just prior to the outbreak of the Crimean War, he would have been conscious of the brutal conflict unfolding around him, as the Russian Army was forced to destroy the fort at Gelendzhik as they retreated from the Ottoman, French and British forces. The result of the war was a crushing blow for the conservative Tsar Nicholas I (1796-1855) and led to the growth of reformist and radical social ideas, thought to have been extinguished during the Decembrist Revolt of 1825. Then, discontented army officers had launched a failed coup against the tsar, and now a new threat loomed for a defeated empire, this time among its youth. It was a threat which was to stalk Nicholas' successor, Alexander II (1818-1881). Having liberated Russia's serfs from bondage in 1861, he was hailed as 'Tsar Liberator' not only for his reforms but also his successful military campaigns on behalf of Orthodox Christians in the Balkans. He overhauled the judicial system and abolished corporal punishment. He promoted local government and expanded university education throughout the empire. With unprecedented access to the increasingly radical ideas emerging from the European left, Russia's institutions of higher learning became the breeding ground for what some would describe as the first terrorist organisation in world history.

Tikhomirov, having turned his back on religion as early as age 10, began to read the radical journal *Russkoe Slovo* (Russian Word) in his teens, absorbing the writings of Nikolai Shelgunov (1824-1891) and Dmitry Pisarev (1840-1868). He was typical of his generation's best and brightest, who set themselves in opposition to the very system which was bringing about the conditions necessary for their education. Having received a gold medal from the gymnasium of

Novorossiysk, he was accepted to study medicine at Moscow University In 1870. By this time, he had become obsessed with politics, and the university served to unite him with like minds.

Anger over the impoverished status of the liberated serfs had led to great anti-establishment sentiment among the country's educated class, fuelling the growth of a *Narodnik* (populist) subculture. Out of this milieu came the Tchaikovsky Circle, named for the revolutionary thinker, Nikolai Tchaikovsky (1851-1926). This self-described 'literary organisation' was in fact a talking shop for revolutionaries who swapped nihilist and anarchist literature between their university lectures. As soon as a Circle started in Moscow, Tikhomirov became a committed member. Time intended for revision was instead spent planning journeys to the rural hinterlands to awaken the peasants and incite a general uprising. At this time, Tikhomirov was gaining a reputation among the would-be revolutionaries as a gifted speaker and, importantly, a brilliant writer. In particular, his revolutionary *shazka* (fairytale), *The Tale of Four Brothers*, was well-received among the Moscow intelligentsia. He also had two further books passed by censors. The efforts of the Tchaikovsky Circle and similar groups to bring revolutionary ideas to the peasantry ended in disillusionment. Generally, the hot-blooded students demanding that agricultural labourers turn against their tsar and their Church were poorly received, not least due to their bungling efforts to take up peasant jobs and adopt the dress of their intended targets. The movement was not yet violent, in large part thanks to the scandal surrounding Sergey Nechayev (1847-1882). Nechayev, the most charismatic proponent of revolutionary violence, whose *Catechism of a Revolutionary* (1869) had radicalised many students, ended up murdering one of his comrades in a paranoid rage and fleeing the country. Having already fallen out with many of the far-left's leading thinkers, his fall from grace put the idea of revolutionary violence in a bad light for many years thereafter.

Peaceful as they initially were, the police soon caught up with the wandering students. Tikhomirov was arrested during a raid on the apartment of a fellow Circle member in 1873. Initially held in preliminary detention (during which he could communicate with nobody), he and his fellow student radicals would not face trial until 1877. The sensational *Trial of the 193* saw unprecedented courtroom theatrics, an unintended consequence of the tsar's legal reforms.

Joined by students rounded up by police in the intervening period, Tikhomirov was one of many who used the trial to propagandise and win over observers to the revolutionary cause. Despite this, he was acquitted. In fact, a great many of the 193 were acquitted, much to the joy of the country's increasingly progressive intelligentsia. Joy quickly turned to anger. Of those imprisoned, some, like Tikhomirov, had been awaiting trial for years only to be acquitted. 38 had lost their minds in captivity, and a further 44 had died, 12 of them by suicide.[1]

A free man by 1878, Tikhomirov petitioned to return to the university, but given his radicalism and floundering academic performance, the application was rejected. Until another opportunity presented itself, politics was his only refuge, and at the time, the prospects for professional revolutionaries seemed bright. The first in a line of revolutionary women, Vera Zasulich (1851-1919), had also just been shockingly acquitted on charges of attempted murder after she shot the governor of St. Petersburg, Fyodor Trepov (1809-1889).[2] The result led to an ever-greater confidence on the part of Russia's political left, and it served to turn the city into a hotbed of revolutionary excitement. Fuel was added to the fire by an economic downturn and the Berlin Treaty, seen by many as a capitulation to Russia's military foes. Tikhomirov soon had his decision made for him when the tsar reversed his acquittal. Faced with the prospect of internal exile, he had no choice but to live life as an outlaw.

During his imprisonment in the Peter and Paul Fortress, Tikhomirov had received several visits by a young woman who would go down in history, Sofia Perovskaya (1853-1881). A member of the St. Petersburg branch of the Tchaikovsky Circle, she was as ambitious as she was ruthless. Bailed out by her rich father, she had not had to endure the confines of prison life in the lead-up to the trial. A brief romance blossomed between the two radicals, but it cooled considerably upon their acquittal. Nevertheless, Perovskaya exerted a lasting magnetism upon Tikhomirov, who had a shy and nervous demeanour whenever he wasn't in the throes of a revolutionary

---

[1] Radzinsky, E. (2006). *Alexander II: The Last Great Tsar*. New York: Free Press, p.256.

[2] While incarcerated, a revolutionary activist, Alexei Bogolyubov (1854-1887) refused to remove his hat for Trepov, who subsequently had him beaten for insolence. This was widely publicised and led to Zasulich's attempt to assassinate Trepov in 1878.

polemic. He had nurtured violent fantasies of a revolution steeped in blood while he lay awaiting trial, and in her zeal to gain similar notoriety to Zasulich, Perovskaya presented him with an opportunity to cross the line into true criminality. An amateur plot cooked up by the couple failed to liberate one of the condemned students, but it did gain them notoriety in the revolutionary underground of St. Petersburg, where they conspired for further action with old and new acquaintances; Andrei Zhelyabov (1851-1881), a handsome career revolutionary from Crimea who exercised a leadership role and eventually became Perovskaya's husband; Nikolai Morozov (1854-1946), the son of a wealthy land-owner; and Anna Yakimova (1856-1942), who had been arrested for subversive activities at a teachers' training school.

Order was brought to this seething underground movement with the re-organisation of *Zemlya i Volya* (Land & Freedom), a long-since defunct revolutionary society given new life by dynamic, young leadership. Key figures included Alexander Mikhailov (1855-1884), Georgi Plekhanov (1856-1918) and Dmitry Lizogub (1849-1879) among others. Land & Freedom was not an avowed terrorist organisation. Too many of its members were still committed to the cause of non-violently inciting an uprising among the peasants, however, it did recognise revolutionary violence as just retribution against the tsar's government for any action taken to suppress it. This explicit stance led to several assassinations by the group's members. The most infamous of the killings was that of the chief of the Third Section (secret police) by Sergey Kravchinsky (1851-1895), who stabbed him to death in the street. A rift in the organisation soon became obvious. On one side, the *villagers*, who felt assassinations would only bring greater clampdowns on their freedom to propagandise, and on the other, *the politicals*, who were increasingly moving to a stance that affirmed terror as the means through which regime change would be achieved. Tikhomirov and Morozov, who edited the group's underground magazine, were in the latter camp, and had the influential Mikhailov on their side.

It was Mikhailov who would be approached by two men willing to give their lives in an assassination attempt against the tsar himself. Grigory Goldenberg (1855-1880), the son of a Jewish merchant, and Alexander Soloviev (1846-1879), an impoverished student. Fearing a general backlash against Jews, Mikhailov took the latter's offer.

This decision almost caused a schism in Land & Freedom, the villagers strongly opposing it, but the deed was done. Two attempts on the tsar's life had already occurred, one undertaken by a disgruntled nobleman, another by a Polish nationalist. Soloviev's effort to shoot the tsar on the morning of April 20th, 1879, met with no more success, but it did seal the fate of Land & Freedom.

A few months later, a secret faction which had taken up the name *Svoboda ili Smert'* (Liberty or Death), met at the spa resort of Lipetsk to discuss their next moves with respect to an upcoming congress of Land & Freedom, set to take place in Voronezh. Eleven members attended, Tikhomirov among them. These eleven made a solemn commitment to terror as a political weapon, one which they would wield, with or without Land & Freedom. Death sentences were to be handed out by a self-selecting *Executive Committee* and sealed with a wax logo featuring a gun, an axe and a dagger. At the head of this committee would be an *Administrative Commission* of three supreme decision-makers: Mikhailov, Tikhomirov and Alexander Kvyatovsky (1852-1880), a rabid supporter of terrorism.

The term 'congress' was itself grandiose. In reality, there were no more than twenty attendees at the Voronezh *congress*, but a constant feature of the revolutionary movement was maintaining the deception that it was multitudinous. At Voronezh, a conciliatory bargain was struck between the moderate and radical factions. Fomenting an uprising was to remain the primary goal, but the congress officially recognised terrorism as necessary. The thoughtful Plekhanov, disgusted by this accommodation of terror, took leave from the movement, while the ranks of the Executive Committee swelled to 25.

In August, Lizogub was unexpectedly arrested and executed in Odessa. On top of the deaths of nineteen others since Land & Freedom's reconstitution, this was the final straw for the terrorist faction. Within days, an amicable divorce was negotiated with the remainder of the villagers, who thereafter adopted the name *Black Partition*, an allusion to their policy of dividing equitably the arable land in Russia. Black Partition was soon dismantled by organisational problems and government arrests, and when its remaining members fled abroad, the clique around Mikhailov gained a monopoly on serious revolutionary activity. The avowed terrorist organisation took the name *Narodnaya Volya* (the People's Will).

Not entirely abandoning the populist credo, the group continued to distribute propaganda to industrial workers and discontented members of the Russian military, much of it written by Tikhomirov. Owing to his mature appearance and erudition, he acquired the nickname 'the Old Man', and his central importance to the party was confirmed in no uncertain terms. His co-editor, Morozov, described him as "the best exponent of our ideas and goals", while Vera Figner (1852-1942), would acknowledge him as the group's "ideological representative, theoretician, and best writer".[3] From Tikhomirov's pen flowed demands for government concessions, demands of "complete freedom of conscience, speech, press, assembly, association, and electoral agitation". Given the entirely unrealistic nature of such requests, there is still debate as to what the organisation hoped to ultimately achieve, and there are indications that this was not even clear among the group's members. Tikhomirov is said to have been the primary member of the *Jacobin* camp which wanted to seize political power from the tsar and use it to implement the revolution by force. This was a view which closely aligned him not only with his old friends, Zhelyabov and Perovskaya, but also with the group's true mastermind, Mikhailov. Referred to as 'the Janitor' due to his extensive knowledge of St. Petersburg's byways and back alleys, Mikhailov was less charismatic than Zhelyabov, but a great deal more intelligent, and his personality complimented Tikhomirov's well. Others in the party objected to any plans for an actual seizure of power and adopted more anarchistic positions. Morozov proved to be the strongest detractor, along with his common-law wife, Olga Lyubatovich (1854-1917). In the end, however, it was Tikhomirov who wrote the party programme, and he assured his comrades that unlike the French Jacobins, they would relinquish power at the earliest opportunity. Unconvinced, Morozov and Lyubatovich later departed for Switzerland, but on the point of primary concern, there was no dissent; the tsar had to die.

Tikhomirov elegantly typed up the death sentence (already agreed upon by all members at the time of the Lipetsk Congress) to be published in August, a practice indicative of the group's desire to appear as a 'government in waiting', whose terrorist acts were akin to government acts, on behalf of *the people*. Even at its height,

---

[3] Ibid. p.307.

however, the organisation never numbered more than 500, including strong sympathisers and hangers-on. Cells existed at a local level across most major cities, and all were dictated to by the members of the Executive Committee.

In November of 1879, attempts were made to derail the tsar's train by mining beneath the railway line and planting explosives, but technical difficulties hampered these early efforts. When the group finally managed to detonate one of their improvised bombs, a stroke of fate led it to harmlessly blow up a luggage car. It was a failure they could scarcely afford, as once the police became aware of the serious threat posed by the terrorists, arrests inevitably followed. Goldenberg's confession under interrogation would have landed the entire cadre in the hangman's noose were it not for the resourceful Mikhailov's spies within the Third Section. Even so, it had its costs. Supplies used in the production of explosives, propaganda, fraudulent papers and the like were discovered and seized. Several revolutionaries did not escape the government's first sweep of the net, Kvyatovsky among them.

On February 5th, another serious attempt was made. A People's Will operative, Stepan Khalturin (1857-1882), having infiltrated the Winter Palace as a joiner, planted explosives beneath the dining room and timed the bomb to detonate as the tsar received a foreign dignitary. Hurrying through a blizzard to Zhelyabov and Tikhomirov, who waited on Palace Square, he only managed to say "it's ready" before a huge blast extinguished the lights of the tsar's home.

"The shatteringly violent sound and the sudden sun-like light were frightening, even to them who expected it. Two and a half stories of the front of the Palace wall were blown outward onto the square across from them [...] They had little doubt that the tsar and his family had been destroyed in the blast."[4]

They were wrong. The bomb only succeeded in killing eleven palace guards.

The foiled assassination plots were plagued by amateurish mistakes, yet time and again the Third Section failed to competently investigate, seemingly giving free reign to the terrorists. Some have speculated that the tsar's internal opponents, disgusted by his

---

[4] Croft, L. (2006). *Nikolai Ivanovich Kibalchich: Terrorist Rocket Pioneer*. Temple, AZ: Institute for Issues in the History of Science, p.71.

dissolute personal life and eager to see his conservative son, Alexander III (1845-1894), take the throne, had no interest in halting the activities of the People's Will. There are facts which hint at this, not least of which is that after the Third Section was dissolved in March of 1880 and replaced by the powerful commission of Count Mikhail Loris-Melikov (1824-1888), the terrorists stopped getting away with their mistakes. The commission had sweeping police powers, and security around the tsar tightened considerably.

Already it seemed that the likelihood of success was slipping through the fingers of the revolutionaries. Greatly disturbed by the failures and the now constant threat of arrest, Tikhomirov asked to leave the organisation, but his oath of loyalty and the persuasion of Mikhailov and Zhelyabov kept him writing for their underground bulletin. It seems that after this incident, however, he was no longer involved in any active plots. While he was a strong proponent of terror in theory, Tikhomirov lacked the nerve required to be a revolutionary criminal. Mikhailov gave him a personal retinue of armed thugs to ensure he felt as safe as possible, but he nonetheless suffered bouts of paranoia, convinced that spies were watching the group's every move. He also began to doubt his own abilities as a propagandist.

By October, the already captured revolutionaries were put on the *Trial of the 16*. Kvyatovsky was condemned to death and hanged in November. The others had their sentences commuted, but never returned to the revolutionary fray, either dying in prison or serving out sentences of hard labour in internal exile. In the same month Kvyatovsky was executed, the greatest disaster struck. Mikhailov was apprehended. The police were now adept at capturing their prey, laying ambushes in the hideouts of those they had already caught. With Mikhailov gone, there was no room for further failure. In defiance of his conservative critics, Alexander II was on the verge of introducing Russia's first constitution, something which would turn the left-leaning public against the radicals. They had one last chance to kill the tsar, and this time, they would need to appear in person.

Having carefully observed the tsar's movements within St. Petersburg, Anna Yakimova opened a fake cheese shop in the basement of Malaya Sadovaya Street, out of which the final plot would be coordinated. Individual bombers with portable explosives would target the tsar's carriage as it passed. Perovskaya was now the driving force behind the People's Will, and she planned for every contingency to ensure they dealt the killing blow. Not even her husband's arrest deterred her. In custody, Zhelyabov snidely informed the officers that nothing they could do would save Alexander II.

On the afternoon of March 13th, 1881, as the tsar's coach travelled alongside the Catherine Canal, it encountered Nikolai Rysakov (1861-1881). Given the signal by Perovskaya, he threw a bomb beneath the carriage. Fortunately for the tsar, it only succeeded in bringing a halt to his journey. The carriage's bulletproof casing had protected Alexander, and the bomb only injured those around it. Rysakov was immediately apprehended. It was at this moment that the tsar made his own mistake, one which cost him his life. Instead of leaving, as his attendants pleaded with him to do, he wavered, demanding to see his would-be assassin. Taking only a few steps away from the shattered carriage, he saw a second man step forth from the smoke.

Ignaty Grinevitsky (1856-1881), a Pole, blew himself up in front of the tsar, becoming the world's first suicide bomber. The blast shattered Alexander's legs, mortally wounding him. As he bled out, he asked to be returned to the Winter Palace, and died there, surrounded by his family, including the son who would succeed him. Alexander III made clear that there would be no mercy for his father's killers.

The gleeful revolutionaries had achieved their aim, but in doing so, the futility of their cause became apparent. Alexander III had been educated by Russia's most strident reactionaries and had no interest in continuing his father's liberal reforms, much less in any kind of constitution. He was a true believer in the autocratic principle, a strongman, and his reign saw the entire swamp of anti-tsarist sentiment in Russia drained, starting with the People's Will.

Perovskaya had placed too much faith in Rysakov. He was nineteen years old and somehow believed he might evade execution if he cooperated with the police. Along with other informants, he helped to identify almost all the leading terrorists. While he knew only faces, pseudonyms and roles, it was enough. Perovskaya and Yakimova, along with their immediate co-conspirators, were arrested. Perovskaya herself did not even manage to escape St.

Petersburg, vainly hoping she might somehow free Zhelyabov from prison.

A statement had been prepared in advance of the tsar's murder, and while Tikhomirov's trembling hand had written it, Zhelyabov had clearly steadied the pen. It denounced Alexander II as a "ravening wolf" who "did not heed the people's tears", who "cared only for the rich", and "hanged and exiled any who stood up on behalf of the people or on behalf of justice".[5] Tikhomirov's true feelings were more accurately reflected in his letter sent directly to the new tsar, an almost apologetic plea for there to be no reprisals against the revolutionaries, and for the tsar to convene a representative body to chart the best course for Russia.[6] However, the Executive Committee was in no position to make demands, and Tikhomirov, the Old Man of 29 years, made plans to flee the country. His paranoia reached new heights, and he affected theatrical mourning of Alexander II in order to deceive everyone he knew, even certain revolutionaries.

In April, Perovskaya, Zhelyabov, Rysakov and two other terrorists were hanged on the parade ground of the Semenovsky Regiment. Mikhailov and Yakimova would have to wait until February of the following year for their own processing in the *Trial of the 20*. They were sentenced to eternal hard labour.

By this time, Tikhomirov and his wife[7] were already in Switzerland, and shortly thereafter, France, having left their daughter with relatives in Russia. Reflecting on the execution of his friends, the haunted exile wrote biographies of Zhelyabov and Perovskaya, Outside of Russia, the terrorist milieu was almost harder to escape, since France was nested with a decade's worth of political runaways. One man in particular acted as an anchor on Tikhomirov, using all means to prevent him surfacing from the revolutionary mire which had turned him into an outlaw and accomplice to regicide. Peter Lavrov (1823-1900) was an older man, a publicist and self-styled philosopher who had been in exile since 1870. He had meant virtually nothing to the People's Will, but after the successful assassination he

---

[5] Ashdown, D. (2009). *Royal Murders: Hatred, Revenge and the Seizing of Power*. Stroud: History, p.178.

[6] Yarmonlinsky, A. (2014). *Road to Revolution: A Century of Russian Radicalism*. Princeton, NJ: Princeton University Press, p.292.

[7] Tikhomirov had married another revolutionary woman, Ekaterina Sergeeva, sometime after 1879. Not much is known about her.

sought any means to gain notoriety through association with the group. Flat broke, Tikhomirov could not afford to turn down the offer of collaborative work writing for a new paper, *Vestnik Narodnoi Voli* (Bulletin of the People's Will), which promised to continue the fight from abroad. This paper had almost no direct connection to the continuing activities of the People's Will in Russia.

With almost all the original members of the terrorist group either dead, imprisoned or in exile, leadership passed to Vera Figner, the last of the founding members still at large. Working with depleted forces, she did not change the organisation's basic orientation, and oversaw the assassination of a secret police agent in Odessa. She eluded capture until December of 1882 when a surprising string of arrests effectively gutted the People's Will for good.

In France, Tikhomirov would have only been vaguely aware of this when, in 1883, he was approached by the young man who had taken over operational leadership from Figner, Sergey Degayev (1857-1921). Degayev tried to convince the exiles to return to Russia, but they were immediately suspicious, and with good reason. There were several inconsistencies in his purported history of arrests and escapes, and the next time he visited, Tikhomirov personally interrogated him, learning that, in fact, he was a police agent under the intimidating sway of the group's most formidable opponent, Georgy Sudeykin (1850-1883), the *inspector of the secret police*.[8]

What followed was an account of a peculiar conspiracy that, while fantastical, is not questioned by most historians. According to Degayev, Sudeykin's intention was not to destroy the People's Will, but to take control of it and use it as a clandestine means to advance his career. Having arrested all of Degayev's competitors for leadership, he would order targeted assassinations of government officials, and the new tsar, fearful of meeting the same end as his father, would appoint Sudeykin as a de facto dictator to combat the threat. He would rule the Russian state while Degayev would rule its underground, and the two would work hand in glove behind the tsar's back.

---

[8] Sudeykin, a former gendarme colonel, had the position of inspector specifically made for him. He was the government's secret weapon, an expert in subterfuge and the use of agent provocateurs.

Whether this conspiracy was genuine, or a ruse tailored to Degayev's youthful naïveté and egoism, it cannot be known for sure, but the result was the same. It was Degayev who had destroyed the People's Will, abusing the trust placed in him by gullible characters such as Figner. The confession forced Tikhomirov to make his last formal decision as a member of the Executive Committee, and given what he knew, it is interesting to ponder whether he made this decision in service to his comrades, or to Russia.

An ultimatum was given to Degayev. He was to return to the homeland and kill his handler. If he refused, the Executive Committee would sign his death warrant. Provided with two revolutionary thugs for the deed, Degayev prepared an ambush in his apartment for the inspector. Due to Sudeykin's physical strength, a surprise attack was the only option. When the inspector arrived with his nephew, Degayev shot him in the back and immediately fled the apartment while his comrades beat the nephew to death with sawn-off crowbars. Neighbours reported the gunshot, but ironically the police were under strict orders not to respond to any disturbances in that particular apartment. Degayev rightly suspected that his comrades had orders to kill him as well. He faked his death and emigrated to the United States where he took the name Alexander Pell. As a much beloved professor of mathematics at the University of South Dakota, his terrorist past was never uncovered during his lifetime. To this day, the university still has a scholarship named after him. Certainly, this was one of the stranger episodes in the history of the People's Will.[9]

Returning to Tikhomirov, his situation was increasingly desperate by 1886. In the political sphere, there was no longer any hope that Russia would see a revolution. The reign of Alexander III was marked by a boom in industrial production and was beset by no military conflicts. He also reversed many of his father's reforms which had provided fuel for the revolutionary underground, including academic freedoms and the power of the *zemstvos* (elected bodies of local administration). Jews and other minority groups were also placed under repressive measures. Pamphlets continued to be printed and young malcontents continued to seethe, but they no longer posed a threat to the government. Attempted terrorist attacks by groups

---

[9] Ibid., p.299.

claiming lineage with the People's Will were easily scuppered by the state. Further, removed from the revolutionary fray, Tikhomirov was often locked in petty, mundane editorial disputes with Lavrov and other members of the emigration whom he despised. On hearing news that his paper, the venture he had invested so much time into at Lavrov's behest, was completely unheard of in Russia, failing to reach even ardent supporters, he sombrely declared that the 'movement' had ceased to even exist.[10]

In his personal life too, Tikhomirov was reaching breaking point. The previous year, he had released a book, *La Russie politique et sociale* (Russia: Political and Social). An impressive and objective sociological study of Russia, it was a work which hardly betrayed his political convictions. Unfortunately, while successful, it did not sell enough copies to keep him out of mounting debt, nor do anything to overcome the constant harassment both from Russian agents and the French police who wished to expel him from the country. He would joke darkly that his landlady would never evict him, given how much she was being paid by spies to monitor his activities. When his son fell ill with spinal meningitis, doctors could do very little, and both Tikhomirov and his wife despaired that their beloved Sasha was to die at any moment.

Miraculously, however, the boy recovered, though his condition remained precarious. Doctors recommended that the Tikhomirovs leave Paris and take an excursion to the small town of Le Raincy, an hour away from the capital, where the air was cleaner. The police gave added encouragement. It was in this small French town that everything changed for the former terrorist.

"Isolated for fifteen months from all that had sustained him in his old views, all that was left of his revolutionary world, Tikhomirov fell back on family life, his love for his wife and son, and finally on the solace of religion. It was as if his past had never existed – the long and agonising road along which he had dissipated his gifts and sacrificed success and personal happiness for a movement which now seemed utterly in ruins".[11]

---

[10] Senn, A. (2008). *The Russian Émigré Press*. Kaunas: Vytauto Didžiojo Universitetas, pp.90-95.

[11] Gleason, A. (1967). The Emigration and apostasy of Lev Tikhomirov. *Slavic Review*, 26(3), pp.423.

He would report an almost mystical transformation attended by a nervous breakdown. Suddenly, he saw the preciousness of life in country walks with his son, meeting stray dogs and finally gaining the courage to show his face at an Orthodox Church. He delved into the Gospels and found himself enraptured by the words of Acts 7:10; "And [God] delivered him out of all his afflictions and gave him favour and wisdom in the sight of Pharaoh king of Egypt; and he made him governor over Egypt and all his house". He ceased to see the tsar as a tyrant, but instead his only chance of salvation. Slowly, he backed away from his fellow revolutionaries.

In 1887, a new preface was added for the second edition of *Russia: Political and Social*. While it did not explicitly repudiate revolution, the message contained therein was confirmation that his position had now changed. Lavrov and others made every effort to stifle and strongarm Tikhomirov into silence after this, fearing what his defection from the cause might mean, but already he was being extricated from their influence. His book's publisher, Albert Savine (1859-1927), was a committed French reactionary and introduced Tikhomirov to circles of high society with a great interest in Franco-Russian relations. Given his new friends and the decision to print the scandalous second preface to his book, all contact within the revolutionary milieu was broken off. Another exile, Nikolai Rusanov (1859-1929) published a denunciation under Lavrov's name entitled *Revolution or Evolution?*

There was, at this point, huge confusion among the emigrant population. It made no sense to them that someone with as great a standing as Tikhomirov, who had written the biographies of their martyred heroes, would betray the revolution. It was unthinkable. To avoid any misconceptions, the *new man* set to work on his answer to Rusanov; *Pochemu ia perestal' byt' revoliutsionerom* (Why I Ceased to Be a Revolutionary*)*, published in 1888. The ink was practically still wet when he submitted it to the assistant minister of the interior in Russia, along with a request for amnesty. He wanted to return home.

In the fall of that year, he was informed by the Russian consul general that his petition was being considered by the tsar himself. A wave of attacks from the left-wing press rained down, all now falling into line behind Lavrov in a delirious panic over what was unfolding. In Alexander III's consideration of amnesty, some would see immediate political motives, the tempting propaganda coup that would be achieved by presenting Russia with a repentant revolutionary. However, it should be remembered that he held Tikhomirov just as personally responsible for his father's gruesome murder as the revolutionaries he had already hanged. When the decision was reached to allow Tikhomirov's return, there was certainly an element of personal forgiveness on the part of the notoriously pious Tsar.

The emigration was furious. Tikhomirov's renunciation of terror was distributed among political prisoners to demoralise them, and the former terrorist's decision to bow at the tomb of the assassinated tsar upon his return was widely publicised. Even so, the loss to the would-be revolutionaries was purely one of prestige. Tikhomirov made his return conditional on never being questioned about his former comrades, and for the remainder of his life, he informed against nobody.

A full pardon was issued in December, with full rights to be restored after five years. His return was timely from a journalistic standpoint. The titan of Russian conservatism, Mikhail Katkov (1818-1887), had just passed. Taking over as editor of the *Moskovskie Vedomosti* (Moscow News), Aleksei Suvorin (1834-1912) reached out to Tikhomirov with the offer of filling Katkov's very large shoes. He would in fact take over as editor himself in 1909, but until then he occupied an increasingly prominent role among the tsar's most vocal backers. He wrote several impressive books reflecting on the problems of Russia; *Beginnings & Ends* (1890), *Social Mirages of Modernity* (1891) *Liberalism & Social Democracy* (1896), *The Religious Composition of Russia* (1902) and *On Monarchist Statehood* (1905), among other works. The final study mentioned here was to be his most grandiose and served as arguably the definitive defence of tsarism. While he adopted an almost monastic devotion to his work, Tikhomirov was an active correspondent with many of the leading conservatives of his day and served as a state advisor. He dined with Tsar Alexander's *éminence grise*, Konstantin Pobedonostsev (1827-1907), and received a golden snuffbox from the tsar's son. He was also very close with the eccentric reactionary philosopher, Konstantin Leontiev (1831-1891)[12], in whom he found

---

[12] We have also translated Leontiev's *Byzantinism & Slavdom*.

a near-perfect mirror of his own thoughts and feelings concerning Russia. Interestingly, the two had planned to collaborate on a secret society of conservatives which would support the regime in clandestine ways (it seems the pull towards covert action had not entirely been extinguished in the Old Man). Alas, Leontiev died not long after Tikhomirov's conversion.

In 1913, the Russian government, besieged by all manner of crises, ceased funding for *Moskovskie Vedomosti*, and Tikhomirov retired, his predictions for the state growing increasingly gloomy. He moved to Sergiyev Posad, away from Moscow's centre. After the Bolshevik Revolution of 1917, he withdrew further, to the grounds of a monastery, and eked out an existence as an underpaid school secretary. His detractors highlighted him to the Soviet authorities, but strangely, they saw no reason to seek revenge on the Old Man, who by now, was in every sense an old man. In fact, the successful revolutionary party did not see much reason to remember the People's Will at all. Vladimir Lenin, despite the fact that his own brother had been executed trying to imitate the terrorists in 1887, remarked on the anniversary of Perovskaya and Zhelyabov's deaths; "they died, so what? Glory and honour to them, but why should we talk about it?"[13]

Tikhomirov died in 1923. His son Sasha, a high-ranking priest, disappeared, like so many Russians after that time.

Both of the works presented here deal with the same subject, a reflection upon how the tracks to disaster for so many youths were laid in 19th century Russia. Without denying the moral culpability borne of free will, Tikhomirov is eager to tease out the social conditions which brought about the loss of the 'cursed generation'. He rejects the revolutionary fatalism which saw radicalisation as an unavoidable, brute fact of the historical process, and instead identifies specific failures both on the part of the Russian state and in particular the intelligentsia. Holding firm to the conviction that Russian liberals

---

[13] Ulam, A. (2018). *Prophets and Conspirators in Prerevolutionary Russia*. London: Routledge, p.393.

paved the way for Russian terrorism, only being too cowardly to follow their own theories to obvious conclusions, Tikhomirov gives us first-hand insight as to the intellectual pressures which faced the youth. This youth, who had been taught what to think, but never how to think, who had been filled with the theoretical dreams of European utopians but were never given a single competent study of the Russian character and the unique social conditions arising from it.

As historical documents, these works are also of interest due to their treatment of the emergence of the first terrorist organisation in world history, the People's Will. While Tikhomirov's observations on terror as a political tactic will come as no surprise to those who have studied the subject, he was perhaps the first to make these observations, given the context. Tikhomirov sees terrorism as futile, the tragic last resort of an entitled few who recognise that the masses they claim to represent do not, in fact, support them. If revolution was truly the *people's will*, terror would be unnecessary, and if it was not, terror would be useless. He justifies this view on the grounds that, if a truly popular movement had no other means at its disposal than terror, then the people in question would be too pathetic to even be worthy of achieving their political aspirations.

In treating the first terrorist organisation, Tikhomirov did not have the data which has come to light since the proliferation of such movements throughout the globe, including the activities of other anarchists and subsequent waves of terror: anti-colonial, new-left, and Islamic. His assertion that terror can never be a winning strategy might seem to be bolstered by failed terror groups such as the Baader-Meinhof Gang in Germany and the Shining Path in Peru, while examples of successful terror campaigns would refute it, including the IRA in Ireland, and the ANC in South Africa. Regardless of the political results, we can be certain that Tikhomirov would condemn all the above as morally evil, not only in light of those they victimised, but also given the debasing effects of terror upon the psyche of its practitioner. He describes life as an *etched wolf*, in constant fear of discovery, of arrest and execution. To dedicate one's life and to sacrifice one's youth to a criminal cause, the nature of which would result in only the severest penalties, was a loss to the entire nation. Tikhomirov felt that the revolutionary movement of his time had committed an unforgivable heist from Russian society, seizing from it those energetic minds which could have improved life for everyone, and instead dedicating them to calculated murder.

In Tikhomirov's Pauline conversion, we find not only an opening of his eyes to the futility of the cause and the wrong-headedness of its leaders, but a genuine embrace of the Russian system of government. He became, in the end, not akin to Plekhanov, who had opposed a general commitment to violence from the beginning, but instead a member of the opposite camp entirely. In his view, the revolutionaries had nothing better to offer the country than its august dynasty, and their zeal for destruction was emblematic of their lack of creative potential. Further, they were victim to their own delusions when it came to both the loyalty which the tsar commanded, and the extent to which he was responsible for the problems facing the country. The liberal intelligentsia offered up the tsar as a sacrificial lamb on the execution block of the revolutionary youth, when all the while it was their own sterility and ignorance of Russia which was failing the people, failing to effectively mature Russian life. The clemency granted to Tikhomirov by Alexander III would have only confirmed his view of the tsar as God's representative on earth, with the power to execute justice as well as forgive the penitent, but not the power to magically alleviate the problems created by an entire stratum of society.

It would also be mistaken to regard the author as having incorrectly assessed the Russian situation, given what we know transpired after the period described herein. This would be to draw too strong a connection between the People's Will and Lenin's Bolsheviks, a connection which even the latter were happy to dismiss. Some will be compelled to see in Russia a kind of *revolutionary tradition*, stretching from the Bolsheviks back to the Decembrists, and perhaps even to earlier peasant and Cossack rebellions in the country's history, but we disagree strongly with such a view. As Tikhomirov himself notes, his generation of student dreamers had an entirely distorted and contrived view of Russian history, imagining themselves to be successors to things which they knew nothing of. Russia's history is turbulent, but the turbulence comes in fits and starts, arising and disappearing in response to the particular conditions of a given time. The emergence of Land & Freedom and the People's Will represents a definite point in the historical timeline; the result of ill-conceived political and legal liberalisation, as well as an irresponsible and immature academia. It was an epoch which rose with the growth of popular education and declined into a bloody finale with the assassinations of Alexander II and Sudeykin. The revolutionary turmoil which afflicted Russia in the early part of the last century was a different animal.

We should note that Tikhomirov is not always forthcoming about the extent of his terrorist past. Given the intention of *Why I Ceased to Be a Revolutionary*, we can understand why he would go to great lengths to paint himself as having always opposed terror, as having been a restraining force within the People's Will. On the contrary, we have no reason to doubt the assertions of others that the pro-terror faction within Land & Freedom was formed on Tikhomirov's initiative. As a publicist, he was not of much use in practical matters. He knew nothing about bomb-making and had no other skills that would have made him indispensable to the plots of the People's Will, but he certainly had full knowledge of them. Despite having ceased active involvement after the failure at the Winter Palace, Tikhomirov's claim that he was kept in the dark about the plot which finally succeeded in killing the tsar seems highly unlikely. And yet, while in his own time the full reality of his involvement in terror would have been an inconvenient truth, it only adds to the weight of his repentance in retrospect.

Some have pointed to the tragedy of Tikhomirov's own life and expressed pity for a man who lurched from one disaster to another, from his own failed revolution to the autocracy that ultimately failed as well. Like two exhausted bears which had hurled themselves at one another, the youth perished, and the state followed. The death of the old Russia was the result. However, while granting that Tikhomirov likely died a "guilt-ridden and unhappy man"[14], we would present the pages contained here as evidence of a personage who finally unburdened himself of a torturous coil.

Tikhomirov's warnings did not save Russia, but they remain a testament to man's capacity to change, to stand at the forefront of an immense, advancing crowd and at least try to prevent it from plunging into the abyss. One can only recall Jeremiah 26; "if you do not listen to the words of My servants the prophets, whom I have sent you again and again even though you did not listen, then I will make

---

[14] Gleason, A. The Emigration and apostasy of Lev Tikhomirov, p.428.

this house like Shiloh, and I will make this city an object of cursing among all the nations of the earth".

Translator's Note

Presented here are Tikhomirov's first two major works after his conversion, *Why I Ceased to Be a Revolutionary* (1888) and *Beginnings & Ends* (1890). The former is the revised edition, which had to have some lines removed to pass censors, and we have included the additions made in 1895 which consisted of some new footnotes, as well as an 1889 newspaper article which Tikhomirov repurposed as a second appendix. This article was in direct response to the torrent of abuse the author received from the Russian emigration.

In translating these works, we have been diligent in ensuring that the author's original intention is reflected in English as clearly as possible. Fortunately, Tikhomirov uses very direct and concise language to get his point across, and as a result we have a great deal of confidence in our translation. All instances of italicisation and bolding in the text are Tikhomirov's.

Note that any dates referred to by Tikhomirov are according to the Julian calendar.

We have included translator's and editor's footnotes to elaborate on both translation decisions and various concepts, events or terms which might be unfamiliar to a contemporary, English-speaking audience.

The greatest thanks to Fin E. for proof-reading, and to Andrej Sennoy for editing and providing footnotes, as well as providing consistent encouragement through a difficult period.

- **K. Benois**

WHY I CEASED TO BE A REVOLUTIONARY

(revised 1888 edition)

Foreword

The following explanation of why I ceased to be a revolutionary was not only written, but in fact published quite some time ago, in 1888.[15]

Unfortunately, this publication had a very sad fate. Some parts of the pamphlet caused its sale in Russia to be censored. My personal circumstances, which made literary activity extremely difficult for almost two years, prevented me from taking timely measures to amend the pamphlet, and when I was finally able to, it seemed to me too late to bother with... So, it remained unknown to the Russian public. I didn't even imagine that, having whipped up a whole storm against me abroad, it could have remained as unknown as I found it to be after two to three years.

However, a few third-party requests, and a particularly kind offer from the editors of *Moskovskiye Vedomosti*[16], prompt me now to do what circumstances did not allow several years ago, that is, to publish, in a revised form, this explanation, which, being my personal one, seems far from devoid of general importance. It goes without saying that I am revising all sections deemed objectionable in 1888. However, I cover everything else, that is to say that I leave, in so many words, the whole body of my explanation as it originally was.

---

[15] In Paris, with the publisher Albert Savine, the then-owner of *Nouvelle Librairie Parisienne*, in the brochure *Pourquoi je ne suis plus revolutionnaire* (it was printed in Russian).

[16] When printing these pages, the editors of *Moskovskiye Vedomosti* included the following note: "Mr. Tikhomirov's explanation, published abroad in 1888, remained completely unknown to the Russian reading public at the time. Now, after the changes in Russian thought during the unforgettable reign of Emperor Alexander Alexandrovich, it is almost more timely than it was in 1888. In light of this, the editors of *Moskovskiye Vedomosti* invited Mr. Tikhomirov to acquaint readers with his considerations from that time." Using this invitation, I published it in serialised form in issues 217, 224, 231, and 238 of the *Moskovskiye Vedomosti* of the current year, 1895.

Of course, in the interests of disseminating my ideas, I could supplement and develop a lot here. But my explanation had a personal, documentary significance for me, and I do not want to give a reason for reproach with any additions, as if I were to present myself to be at least somewhat different from what I was. In reality, of course, there is nothing different to present. Not to mention that it would be hard to accuse me of fearing to be myself. But, in addition, 1888 was the moment when my worldview finally matured, which determined all my subsequent literary activity, and which I further developed in *Beginnings and Ends* (1890), *Social Mirages* (1892), *The Struggle of the Century* (1895) and a number of other articles.

All the foundations of this worldview are not difficult to see in the following explanation of 1888. But I can admit without false shame that the development of this worldview was not easy for me. A lot of time was required for me to understand its particulars. This was inevitable, given its genesis.

From my early youth I learned a completely different worldview, which then dominated the "progressive" strata of Russian society. Like everyone else, I adopted these views even before I had any independent observations of life, any independent criticism, or even a mind ripe enough for such things. Having some ability to write, I, like the vast majority of today's liberal and radical writers, for many years remained a compiler of other people's thoughts, taken on faith, considered wise because *everyone* said they were, and this approach affects all writings in the mass of historical, economic etc. essays. Like everyone infected with this "progressive" worldview, I learned about life first from books. The unnatural dominion of the book, one must confess, is now a great evil. The number of facts personally observed, the number of sensations directly experienced, almost everyone now considers such things negligible when compared with what is grasped from the abnormally trumpeted process of reading. The "wisdom" and "sensation" found in books held me in their power for many years.

It was only thanks to the special conditions of my life, those that almost forced me to directly observe the facts of human relations and therefore directly experience the real sensations they generated, that I gradually became critical of the current views of the progressives. My criticism being, as it were, an involuntary concession to a blatant, clamouring fact, thus went from a *specific* to a general conclusion. It

2

was a slow and difficult road; each step of it cost me dearly, especially since I travelled alone, and I had a long wait before a *general* idea appeared in front of me, rewarding my consciousness for a series of losses and disappointments. Developing from the specific to the general, my thinking was first of all compelled to discard the obvious insignificance of purely revolutionary ideas, and then this radius expanded to encompass an ever-larger portion of the "progressive" worldview. But then where could I hang my hat? How much of this ground consisted of an unquestionable lie, and where, perhaps, did at least relative truth begin; this was not immediately clear to me. In this regard, the year 1888 constitutes an era, the moment, of the final revolution.

The reasons why I published this pamphlet in 1888 were outlined in its preface, but for the modern public they require a more detailed exposition. The fact is, my long-standing efforts to eliminate the "terrorist" idea among the revolutionaries remained completely unsuccessful. On the contrary, by 1888, this immoral and ludicrous idea began to manifest itself with increased persistence. In view of this, I considered it necessary to oppose it as decisively as possible. The first opportunity for this came in the form of a new edition of my book *La Russie Politique et Sociale*, which gained notoriety abroad and, as I knew, among Russian radical elements. As a matter of fact, this book, in my opinion, required a huge alteration. But the opportunity did not materialise. The publisher who ordered the reprint did not agree to the changes and provided only a *foreword* to use as I wished.

I used the foreword to outline the weakness of the revolutionary idea. By the same token, I needed to answer some of the criticism I had received, and it seems that some aspects of my answer have not yet lost their significance for a certain part of our intelligentsia.

Here is what I wrote in lieu of a foreword, starting with a comment from the London magazine *Atheneum*:

"The English magazine, in an article so flattering to me, expresses the idea that the exaggerated demands[17] of the Russian intelligentsia only slow down the advance of freedom. It seems to me that this opinion is based on a distorted apprehension of reality.

---

[17] About which I treat in this book.

3

I believe that it is not the breadth or narrowness of the demands that has led to the powerlessness of the Russian liberal movement. The real reason for the powerlessness of our political programmes is that they are too theoretical, too unrelated to the national, too little calibrated for the conditions of our country. The fragile culture of Russia has not yet had the time to accumulate a sufficient number of political and social observations drawn from the life of the country itself.

The man of the Russian intelligentsia sharpens his mind primarily with foreign books. Thus, he creates a purely deductive worldview for himself, a purely logical construction, where everything exists in great harmony, except for the foundation; something which remains completely brittle. Thanks to the worldview which springs forth from this, people in Russia are now able to stubbornly demand the implementation of things which are entirely impracticable or of no serious significance, and at the same time leave neglected the conditions of paramount importance.

Under Emperor Nicholas I, the government undertook the reorganisation of the state's peasantry. To enact his ideas, the emperor chose well Count Kiselyov[18], one of the greatest statesmen that Russia ever gave birth to. Thus, one of the most remarkable social organisations in our history was created. All of the regions in Europe were taken into the hands of the state, the peasants were abundantly endowed, and the resettlement system gave rise to new generations of the agricultural class; a wonderful, national food system emerged to combat crop failure; the improvement of agricultural practice among 20 million peasants became the subject of the conscious, mandated work of the ministry. Moreover, the peasants were personally free, and their communities were governed by people they chose. After two decades of effort, this vast organisation finally rose to its feet.

1861 approached. Alexander II undertook the liberation of serfs. The situation of state peasants was then more than satisfactory. Their crop was successful, they paid taxes correctly, their previous tendency towards riots disappeared or faded. What could have been

---

[18] **(Ed.)** Pavel Kiselyov (1788-1872): Imperial Minister of State Properties from 1837 to 1855. State peasants were personally free, while remaining tied to the land, this land falling under the administration of the Russian state.

4

easier than to imitate this happy example and expand the scope of the already created organisation? Yet what did we do? From 1858 to 1861, countless words were spoken, ranging from freedom to socialism, and for what? To end the disruptive reforms of February 19th."

Given this historical example of the fact that our undertakings do not always suffer from excessive *breadth* of demands, since in this case the people of 1856-1861 were unable to capture the breadth of the idea of the "Nikolaev" era, I continue:

"Rather than a narrower focus, it is the acquisition of greater maturity that we require. We need to get rid of our primitive, childish imagination, which enjoys fireworks and sparkling phrases. It is necessary for us to cultivate the imagination of a mature, developed people who cleave to a solid structure based on the unshakeable facts of reality. In other words, this means that we need to develop civilisation and science as soon as possible, and further, must give particular attention to the study of our country and people. We need to become able to independently chart our course, and if we achieve this, no breadth of needs will harm us."

After this general discussion, I turned to the question of "revolutionary extremes," in which the primary narrowness of thought reaches its outer limit, especially in the form of *terrorism*.

"I will not," I say, "touch on the moral aspect of such systematic actions, although I foresee serious moral dangers in establishing a habit of ruling on the very lives of human beings, based solely on one's own discretion. But this is not the point. Even restricting ourselves to an analysis of the political issue, from this point of view the terrorist idea should be recognised as absolutely false.

One of two things is true: either there are forces which will overthrow this regime, or there aren't. In the former case, there is no need for political killings, in the latter, they will lead to nothing. The idea of intimidating a government without having the power to overthrow it is completely chimerical: governments so remarkably unintelligent do not exist in this world. As for the fear of death, it stalks one's person in wartime, yet how many generals have surrendered because of it?

Either it is unnecessary or powerless; this is the sole dilemma faced by terrorism as a systematic method of political struggle. We don't even mention here the danger posed by its effect on the mind, in which great social issues are constantly obscured by demeaning clashes with investigators...

I am afraid that the consequences of this humiliation are already having an effect. How often I encounter people who do not expect anything great for the future of Russia, nothing but some parliament, some liberties, and to achieve these trifles, they pin their hopes on murders and violent measures...

In my opinion, everything is false in this deplorable assessment of things. First of all, its pessimism, because if there is a country from which the magnificent development of a distinct culture can be expected, then this, of course, is Russia. Secondly, pinning hopes on political killings betrays a complete misunderstanding of how society works. A dagger and dynamite can only confuse every situation to which they are applied. Ideas alone can illuminate; healthy, positive ideas, able to show Russia not how to shed blood, but how to cultivate strength. You must have a creative idea, a socially constructive idea. Only then is it worth talking about political liberties."

This brief series of thoughts was, in fact, what provoked a passionate campaign against me by revolutionaries who had no shame in using anything at their disposal to destroy me. They were especially indignant at how I dared to openly declare a change in my views. "Couldn't you keep your mouth shut," I heard from all sides. I answered with the pamphlet *Why I Ceased to Be a Revolutionary*, which I reproduce authentically on the following pages.

This pamphlet had two appendices, whose contents, with additional explanations, I now set out in *Appendix No. 1*.

In addition, I place in *Appendix No. 2* my answer to the emigrant polemic against me, since this answer is a natural addition to the 1888 pamphlet. It was printed in the *Moskovskiye Vedomosti* in 1889.

- **September 2, 1895**

Part I

If my scepticism regarding the various foundations of our revolutionary worldview had been lying dormant, then it surely would have been roused at this point, when I observe with such clarity the ease and speed with which the revolutionary direction has become fully ossified like Old Belief.[19] Every phenomenon, of course, ends in death, and before reaching this stage it undergoes a period of senility, mineralisation. But this has come on so quickly, before anything has even been done, before it has even emerged from the chaos of internal contradictions, in a word, before it has even taken shape; something which no doubt shows how devoid of vitality the seed of the phenomenon was. I observe this reality in several, separate areas, but they remind me of numerous analogies.

My confidence that I am now on the right track only grows when I listen to the reproaches that are heard against me and observe actions that it will be more useful to talk about sometime posthumously, in the pages of what becomes 'Russian Antiquity'.

These people reproach me with a thousand things: why didn't I speak out before, why didn't I remain silent, why didn't I wait, why did I leave the party, etc. There is no point in answering most of these reproaches, because they simply reflect the difference in point of view on the moral rights and duties of a person. I only note that in this regard, in fact, I have not changed at all and appear the same as I always did. There is, however, something to be answered for.

They reproach me: why didn't you keep quiet? They say to me: you must be silent... I know this reflects a common occurrence: many who have reached an age of experience cease to believe in their former foundations and dreams; yet they are silent! They do not share their experience with young people, resolving: "why disappoint

---

[19] **(Ed.)** Old Belief is a schismatic Orthodox sect which emerged in opposition to the Church reforms carried out between 1652 and 1666 under Patriarch Nikon of Moscow (1605-1681). The division, known as *Raskol*, persists to this day.

them? You might do nothing yourself, but don't disturb others!" There are those for whom the reasons for loyalty to what they previously believed lies in an inner cry of regret for lost life: "How can it be that truly, these five or ten years were a mistake? This thing into which I put so much effort, for which I gave up this and that… It cannot be!" This situation is deeply tragic; it cannot but arouse pity. But, recognising the causes of such cowardice and even personally forgiving those who fall victim to it, we must not forget that it bears a heavy responsibility for the ruin of our vital youth, for the futility of our "movements". I consider it a duty to do otherwise. When I believe something was right, I say yes; when I think not, I say no. I wrote programmes at twenty; now that I am almost forty, I'd hold myself in very poor regard if I were afraid of my twenty-year-old writings or could not say anything more intelligent now. Whether anyone will listen to me is a different question, but my duty is perfectly clear.

Regarding the reproaches for my attitude towards the so-called 'Party of the People's Will', I also wish to establish the facts once and for all, so as not to leave room for slander or error.[20]

There are two kinds of duties: moral, prescribing that we do what our conscience indicates, and formal, prescribing that we do what we are obligated to do. Subordinating them, of course, to moral duties, I nevertheless fully recognise my formal responsibilities. But the fact is that in relation to the former 'Party of the People's Will' I cannot be blamed for violating even formal duties. I supported her much longer than common sense, my beliefs and my responsibilities to my homeland allowed.

Once, I welcomed the appearance of this party, I gave to it all my strength. I was still a revolutionary then, but I already understood the necessity of creation, without which a healthy movement cannot exist. In the new movement, I imagined something creative, the elements of which I tried to instil in it to the fullness of my understanding. Thus, faithfully, in conscience and conviction, I served almost until the end of 1880. At this point I, and not I alone, began to feel that there was in fact no creative power in this movement. I went through the whole year of 1881 with a purely

---

[20] They reproached me as if I had left their "party", whereas I, in fact, did not necessarily belong to the "party" of that time.

formal "fidelity to the banner". At the time I felt perplexed. Russia was healthy; this was my impression; the country was full of vitality; but then why was the revolutionary movement withering away, this thing which was, as my theories informed me, the highest manifestation of the country's development?

This seemed to me an incredible contradiction that I could not resolve, and which led me to a kind of cold despair. So, I went abroad, with only the desire to write my memoirs.

I note in passing that I left with the consent of my comrades, but without any instructions, being in general completely free, warning that I would be gone for an indefinitely long time. During this "indefinite vacation" of mine, there, in Russia, all the remnants of the old organisation collapsed, everyone died in relation to whom it would be possible to speak accurately about my *obligations*.

My time abroad would indeed be long, and I don't really have any right to discuss the circumstances which led to this, considered apart from my other behaviour abroad. I will say one thing: it was the most abhorrent time of my life.

This was the only opportunity that the circle, using all the manpower at its disposal, had to restrain and suffocate me. Of course, there were reasons for this, and to comply was a duty, a routine party duty, which for something still living would have constituted a vivifying action, but in the case of a dying movement, it reminds one of sins punishable up to the seventh generation. Reality gave me terrific directions. But in order to make use of such things, one must have a freely functioning mind and conscience, one must allow themselves to think and feel, and yet such allowances don't exist in parties, especially not in ours. I consoled myself with the thought that, being in the ranks of the party, I would better contribute to its reformation. What self-seduction! It turned out, of course, that I only subordinated myself, that I remained silent by thinking much less than I should have, and even preventing others from thinking.

Despite, however, the full consciousness in which I castrated my mental abilities, I could only achieve a slowdown in my development, unable to halt it completely. Life worked too intelligently. I could not help noticing her instructions. The activities of German Lopatin[21] and

---

[21] **(Ed.)** German Lopatin (1845-1918): Revolutionary publicist and chief go-between for the members of the People's Will in Russia and those in the

his comrades gave me a new warning. I observed that they were not doing what was needed. What was needed I couldn't definitively discern from abroad, but I strongly advised G. Lopatin to look for new ways, since the old ones in which he was set were obviously futile. When I saw that he and his comrades either lacked the knowledge or will to depart from the old ways, I (in the summer of 1884, I don't remember the exact date) wrote to G. Lopatin personally, that he should no longer consider me a member of the circle, and shouldn't make use of my name again.

Since then I have withdrawn from all sorts of circles and organisations. Occasionally I had the impulse to start something new; but already here I was not subordinate to any parties.

Now, if readers allow, I reproduce a few excerpts from my diary for 1886. In March of that year, I note that in my circumstances (which had come about, please note, in January 1885), "I was finally convinced that revolutionary Russia (in the sense of a serious, creative force) does not exist... There are revolutionaries, they move and will move, yet they do not represent a storm but rather ripples on the surface of the sea... They can only slavishly repeat practices... They don't even adopt anything from their forebears except for appearance and technique". Further: "In my eyes, for over a year it has been certain that from now on we must expect everything only from Russia, from the Russian people, and expect virtually nothing from the revolutionaries". I concluded from this that "I must arrange my life in such a way as to be able to serve Russia in the way that my instinct tells me, apart from any parties".

These are the facts. Readers can see that for a long time I have had absolutely no obligations with respect to the Party of the People's Will. If there are individuals who would like to resurrect it[22] ; what does this have to do with me? It obliges me to nothing. Such an attempt was not mine, and on the contrary, I always advised against it, made clear that I did not approve of it and that it would only bring harm to Russia. The question of how one or another of the deceased representatives of the old movement would react now, is interesting to me in the historical and psychological sense but cannot have any

---

emigration. He was arrested in 1884 upon trying to return to the country and would remain in prison until 1905.

[22] They then tried to resurrect it, hence why they were especially angry with me for my open renunciation of all revolutions. (*1895 note*).

influence on the path I have chosen. I could allow my mind to sleep again, and upon their resurrection and pronouncement, give them my obedience. However, if today any people should rise from their graves, no matter how close they were to me, I would do only one thing: use all my strength, all my knowledge, all my reasoning to convince these people to come with me. And then, with or without them, I would still go my own way, the way I consider true.[23]

---

[23] These lines are written in response to the reproach of emigrants that I am betraying my "old comrades", their "graves".

Part II

There are many of my peers who were similarly given lessons from life, and nevertheless continue to passively "hold the banner", driving away with horror the thought of any changes, especially towards "moderation". To discard the habits of so many years and to go so far as to completely cease to be a revolutionary, it seems to them something beyond human reason. I saw otherwise. Why? The reasons, of course, are many. Incidentally, I was obliged in the extreme sense to observe French life, something which showed me the truly precious aspects of culture and the paltry profit of revolutionary ideals. The most important thing to recognise is that there are two sides to dreams of revolution. One is the more seductive aspect of destruction, the other is the desire to create something new. In me, it was the latter which long prevailed. In general terms, I would be personally quite interested in tracing the outline of my *present* self in my revolutionary past, through which I might gratefully look at my pre-revolutionary years. Regardless of everything, these years of upbringing imparted to me a personality which even the stream of progressive ideas that flooded our generation could not completely erase. Of course, I do not intend to treat the reader with my autobiography. I simply relate here that the fully established ideas of public order and strong state power long distinguished me within the revolutionary environment; I never lost sight of Russia's national interests and would always have laid down my life for the unity and integrity of Russia. In my socialism, I could never join any particular school. Regarding rebellion, I dreamed of the barricades, then of conspiracy, but I was never a "terrorist".[24]

A certain imprint of positivity lay over my revolutionary attitude.

In general terms, I would divide the revolutionary period of my life into three phases:

---

[24] **(Ed.)** There is some embellishment by Tikhomirov here, understandable given his strong desire to be allowed to return to Russia.

13

1) dreams of raising the masses (the era of 'Land & Freedom'), and while never considering imposture and dishonesty, I thought, so to speak, of "honest rebellion";

2) dreams of a coup d'état through a conspiracy, and in so dreaming I was willing to tolerate terror, though I tried to curb it and subordinate it to creative ideas (the era of the 'People's Will');

3) dreams of a coup d'état through a conspiracy, but by now sharply condemning terror and demanding instead greater cultural work (the era of the demise of the 'People's Will').

In the wake of this, I abandoned the revolution itself, in a general sense. Like the first two, the third phase is now also an element of my past. However, it is one which is less known to the public (that is, in their assessment of me), since at that time I wrote almost nothing. It will prove useful to restore the physiognomy of who I was then. I have a completely objective document with which to do this: an article that was not allowed to be published in *Bulletin No. 5 of the People's Will.*

I regret that the lack of space does not allow me to reproduce it here in its entirety. Its essential points are as follows.

Russia, I declare, is in the most ordinary, so to speak, normal state, while the revolutionary parties are in disarray. Such a discrepancy can be explained only by the errors in the party programme.

"The programme of the People's Will was merely an attempt," I write. "In order to become a truly Russian revolutionary programme, it would need to be revised and corrected twenty times with the help of the cultural-revolutionary movement it should have roused [...] The party should not stand on its own, nor defend itself, but, on the contrary, become one with Russia".

It turned out that all of this was beyond the understanding of the revolutionaries. Right away, the 'People's Will' made such a huge mistake as including destructive and terroristic activities in its programme. Subsequent years only saw this intensify. I lay this out in great detail in the article, from the point of view of a conspirator. My rejection of terror is extremely harsh. "If they told me that in any given country, there were no methods left but resorting to terror, I would seriously doubt the ability of this country to survive". However, terrorism was precisely what was being developed to ever greater extents within the party, completely undermining its forces, its preparatory work, even while "the role of the true revolutionaries is not simply one of rebellion, but a cultural role as well".

The idea of terror narrowed and impregnated the idea of revolution from all sides, made its business the exclusive property of "its" people (too often criminals), and thus it prevented the party from becoming a broad social movement. I conclude the article with a reminder that all disappointments unfold in the midst of the party itself. "Russia, in a broader sense, is going its own way". It must therefore be hoped that "Russia and its intelligentsia will learn to understand each other," and therefore I boldly toasted the readers, "to a better future".

Such was how I wished to appeal to the readers of the *Bulletin* in its farewell issue, in the summer of 1886. However, the editors and publishers unanimously, and with some horror, found my article to be inappropriate, saying I had no right to publish it in the 'Bulletin of the 'People's Will''. So, it was lost.[25]

I was very indignant at that time: it seemed to me incredible how people might not understand that I was showing them the only serious, reasonable way forward, which, moreover, as it seemed to me, only developed the best dreams of the old time, only more mature and stronger.

It was a perfectly legitimate sentiment. But, on the other hand, I can't help but confess now that the rationality of my action and the spirit of vitality manifested in it ought to have taken a further logical step and completely discarded the "revolutionary path of action". After all, I myself claimed in the article that "only a certain evolution in public life can create the basis for revolutionary activity". I demanded the unity of the party with the country. I demanded the banishment of terror and the development of a "great national party"... But then what good were conspiracies, rebellions, coups?

Such a party, the creation of which I imagined, would obviously be able to develop a system of improvement that was at the same time quite possible and clearly fruitful, and as such would find the energy and aptitude to present itself to the government, which in turn could not ask for more than to spearhead the reform itself.

---

[25] Actually, only the second half (ten pages) were lost, these being the pages with "profanity".

As such, my point of view was indeed dangerous and heretical for those who wished to be revolutionaries at all costs. It was dangerous because, in the end, it departed from the revolution (even though this was its starting point). It was heretical because, consciously or unconsciously, it was imbued with the spirit of denial when faced with the many foundations of revolutionary faith.

We (and not we alone) truly imbibed this deeply rooted idea that we lived in some kind of "period of destruction", which, as they still believe, was to culminate in a terrible coup with rivers of blood, the crack of dynamite, etc. Then, it was supposed, the "creative period" would begin. This social concept, itself a kind of political reflection of the old ideas of Cuvier[26] and the school of sudden geological catastrophes, is completely wrong. In fact, in real life, destruction and creation go hand in hand with one another, and are unthinkable apart. In fact, the destruction of one phenomenon occurs because something else has burst forth from it, in its place, and, conversely, the formation of the new is nothing but the destruction of the old. Whoever has the power to destroy while lacking the power to create the new immediately, brings only necrosis to a part of the social organism. However, in most cases and under such conditions, the destruction itself is purely fictitious: a man destroys, for example, a person, while the idea, the estate, the institution he represents, continues on in strength and health.

In our country, this revolutionary destruction constitutes the faith, hope, and duty of every good radical. Everything that constitutes rebellion, subversion, overthrow, is considered as something useful, containing a grain of progress. Destruction is considered all the more useful if it is directed against the administration or government, that is, against the very centre which protects the existing order. The idea of instigating riots, rebellions, conspiracies of all kinds, tried to come into being through us in a variety of ways, but it found no success in any of them: there was no "material" in Russia for the barricades, for insurrection, for conspiracy, that is to say, there was no sympathy or desire for it on the part of the people and society.

---

[26] **(*Ed.*)** Georges Cuvier (1769-1832): French naturalist and founding father of palaeontology. After establishing extinction as a scientific fact, he became the most prominent proponent of the catastrophist idea of history, that all history is shaped by sudden, violent events.

Under such conditions, the only real option for manifesting the uprising, with the exception of the ill-fated student unrest, was the individual revolt, that is, terrorism. For this method of action, there is never a need for either the support or sympathy of the country. One's conviction, one's despair, one's determination to die are enough. The less a country wants a revolution, the more natural it is for those who want to stay on a revolutionary footing at all costs to resort to terror, crafting a cult of revolutionary destruction. Apologists for political assassination very rarely, I suppose, realise that the real power of terrorism in Russia stems from the hopelessness of the revolution; but when faced with this reality they only strive more stubbornly for terror, even despite the efforts of the most gifted people in their own camp.

Terrorism will disappear when the idea of acting upon the revolutionary path disappears. Unfortunately, the idea of a revolutionary path is raised up through all the weaknesses of Russian education. The demand for intensified cultural work which fell directly upon this weak point was, regardless of my own wishes, anti-revolutionary. The very fact of its formulation stands as an indication that, in my mind, the revolution had already been unconsciously laid to rest.

So, I give just treatment to those who rejected my article. As revolutionaries, they were right to do so. But I, I too was right, as a man whose thought went further and deeper. I had only one error then: I did not dare to part with some remnants of the rebellion and with the very word "revolution", a term which has been co-opted by far too many insurgents for it to beneficially serve any rational programme.[27] I soon corrected this error.

---

[27] I must still remind P. Lavrov, along with all of my opponents, that the word "revolution" is understood not only as a violent coup, upon which their imagination is fixed, but also as something entirely different, namely the process of changing a phenomenon, even if this change occurs quite peacefully. In such a scientific sense of the word, some say, for example: Christianity accomplished through peaceful evolution the greatest revolution in the world. My revolutionism was looking for precisely this evolution, this historical process of changing the nature of a thing, in order to act in accordance with it. P. Lavrov, like his comrades, aspires not to simply find this nature, to strengthen the process of its development, but instead to seek out revolutionary paths and means of action, that is, a fight, a rebellion, destruction. They are all, of course,

The revolutionary period of my thinking has come to an end and passed into eternity. I did not abandon my ideals of societal justice. They only became more modest, clearer. But I also concluded that violent coups, riots, destruction (all this being a painful product of Europe's crisis) would be not only fatal, but impossible for Russia. This is not our disease. We only have something bookish, grafted on, inculcated by the absence of the Russian intelligentsia. But one should not attach importance to it either. Of course, our revolutionary movement does not have the power to tear Russia from the path of her historical development, but it remains a great harm, slowing down and distorting this development.

I cannot go into detail in terms of a critical analysis of the many intertwined, often opposing points of view that make up the theoretical baggage of the revolutionary movement. In fact, I need only lay out my own attitude towards it. I therefore dedicate the following pages to only three questions, those which have the greatest practical importance:

- That of terrorism.
- That of student unrest.
- That of my assessment of the forms of government.

---

gratefully justified by the fact that it seems impossible to act without destroying this or that. This is a mistake, and one I cannot recommend anyone commit. I will ask: is the evolution on which they base their proposal to change a nature even present in the county? If so, and if they seized upon it, then they would have been able to act, and could obviously have done what the country was doing even without them. If there is no such evolution, then there is nothing to say on the subject of revolution. Such conclusions are reached when trying to give the word "revolution" a serious sociological meaning. (*1888 note*).

Part III

The idea of *terror* is in itself so pathetic that one doesn't even feel like talking about it. What I said in the preface to *La Russie politique et Sociale* is perfectly true: terrorism, as a system of political struggle, is either powerless or unnecessary: it is powerless if the revolutionaries have no means to overthrow the government, and redundant if such means exist. Meanwhile, it is harmful in both the moral and psychological sense. I said this very softly in that introduction. The architects of the outcry against me[28], however, have attacked with particular vehemence on this point, and it must be acknowledged that the "old heathens", as they call themselves, can still influence young people today, since they flatter points of view they already hold. Therefore, I will express my thoughts more fully.

The "old heathens" recall the well-worn argument in favour of terror, that it "disorganises the government". I myself argued in the above-mentioned article (included for the 'Bulletin of the 'People's Will'') that it, above all, "disorganises the revolutionaries themselves". As for the government, I would like to see in precise wording exactly how this "disorganisation" manifests. I myself once agreed with this argument, but what seemed like a sign of disorganisation before 1884, in my opinion, completely evaporated later.

In general, my own observations led me to the conclusion that, while the political assassinations had caused the government a certain amount of frustration for as long as they imagined there to be some formidable force opposing them, as soon as they realised that the very reason for the assassinations was that this was the work of an insignificant handful, they, in my opinion, showed no further signs of frustration. They mastered a solid, systematic way of dealing with the problem and proceeded without a moment's hesitation. Without a doubt, the personal lives of government officials capable of inciting

---

[28] That is, the emigrants who protest against me.

the hatred of terrorists have been extremely corrupted by the constant expectation of assassination attempts. But of course, no matter how unpleasant such a life is, no one will surrender because of it. Firstly, it would be a demonstration of the utmost cowardice, and secondly, it would entail too much danger in the future. If they were to give in to the socialists today, in fear for their own lives, seeing this, the serf-owners will issue the same threats to extract concessions tomorrow, and the day after, the large capitalists will follow, etc. The whole thing would be too pointless...

In this aspect, that is, in the sense of political change, the significance of terror is approximately zero. But below this level, it is reflected in the most harmful effects, on the revolutionaries themselves and everywhere their influence reaches. It fosters complete contempt for society, for the people, for the country, fosters a spirit of egoism, incompatible with any social system. In a purely moral sense, what power can be greater than the power of one person over the life of another? This is a power which many (and not the worst by any means) would refuse even to society itself. And so this power is appropriated by a handful of people, who do not kill to avenge any atrocities, to avenge anything that would put their intended victims beyond the limits of humanity; they kill, so to speak, to avenge a political crime. And what is this political crime? The fact that the legitimate government, recognised by the people, does not wish to fulfil the self-proclaimed demands of a handful of people who are so deeply aware of themselves as an insignificant minority that they do not even attempt an open struggle with the government.

Of course, from these people you can hear a lot of phrases about "returning power to the people". But these are nothing more than empty words. After all, the people are not asking for this in any sense, and instead, are constantly discovering their readiness to cave in the heads of their "liberators" for it. Only the desperate romanticism of the revolutionaries allows them to live in such fictitious ways and to trample on Russian power, as it would be permissible to trample on the power of some usurper. The Russian tsar does not steal power; he receives it from the solemnly chosen ancestors, and still the people, with all their multitudes, in any case show their readiness to support with all their might the cause of their great-grandfathers.

Who turns out to be a tyrant here? Is it not the revolutionaries, who, recognising themselves as an insignificant minority, have allowed themselves to raise a hand against the monarch, who represents the whole nation and is responsible to nobody, but was consecrated by the Church with the title of its secular head?

They may object to me that the question of legality is not always appropriate, that sometimes, self-proclaimed rebels are morally more representative of the people than their legal representatives. It happens. But in order to imagine this about ourselves, *facts* are needed, and the facts of the history of our ill-fated movement are such that now, I can no longer explain the illusion of "moral representation" even by means of the vividness of imagination, but must attribute its persistence to its inertia and immunity to all impressions. Are all the classes of the country still not shouting loudly enough that the revolutionaries are "renegades" for these people?

Anarchists also like to refer to the theory of "natural", inherent human rights. However, one cannot fail to notice that the question of natural human rights is, to some degree, controversial; theoretically, they become clear only when the nature of society is fully established. In practice, they become clear only when "natural rights" are recognised by law (such as in the American or French declaration of human and civil rights). We have had nothing of the kind, and the revolutionaries themselves in their programme did not proceed at all from "natural rights" but from the "people's will". And yet, the "people's will" is for the government to decide, and for us to submit to. But even if "natural rights" had formed the basis of the programme of any party, this would not give it any licence for political assassinations, which undoubtedly constitute an encroachment on individual freedom and the rights of society.

On the whole, terrorism, the practice of political assassination, is a system of struggle that has not only failed to uncover a right to exist, but even a right for its idea to exist. In reality, such an idea can only be an anarchist declaration of the individual's omnipotence and contempt for the power of society. But, in educating entire generations with such ideas, terrorism does not even have the logic of anarchism, and somehow manages to publicly renounce anarchy, requiring centralisation, discipline... Is this not, in general, a true school of randomised thoughts, a school that accustoms people to activities not comprehended by any broad sociological outlook?

21

The degrading effect of terrorism, therefore, is inevitable, even if we disregard the fact that it often boils down to a "brawl" of urban thieves. The architects of the outcry are offended that I describe this "brawl" as *abaissante*; degrading. But even so! I also understand these skirmishes as minor episodes. However, when the fight against the police and attempts on the lives of government officials become the movement's basis, this undoubtedly lays low those involved, relegating them to a status far below that of reformers. The reformer, if he is not an impostor, must stand, intellectually and morally, above the environment into which he brings light, and so possess the power to reshape and influence it. Such is his pride and power. What can I say if such an influence, such "cultural work", begins to seem quasi-performative, even completely impossible[29], and the terrorists themselves, without a twinge of conscience, admit that they can act only with daggers and false passports?

The influence of the terrorist conspirator's very lifestyle is extremely numbing. This is the life of an etched wolf. Above all, there is the consciousness of the fact that not only today or tomorrow, but every second he must be ready to die. The only way to live with such a consciousness is not to think about a great many things, which, however, you need to think about if you want to remain a cultured person. Attachment of any serious kind is, in this state, a true misfortune. The study of any issue, social phenomenon, etc. becomes unthinkable. A plan of action which would be more or less complex, more or less extensive, they daren't allow to enter their mind. Everyone, without exception (save five to ten like-minded persons), must be deceived from morning to night, be hidden from, be suspected as an enemy in every case... Especially outstanding energies are needed in order to at least be able to work and think a little with such an unnatural life. And such people, if they do not break free from the sucking swamp of their surroundings, quickly sink. For people of a lower calibre, the incessant affairs with spies, false passports, safe houses, dynamite, ambushes, dreams of murders, escape plans; is much more fatal.

---

[29] The words of the terrorists were, "nothing can be done". (*1895 note*).

Part IV

The second manifestation of our "revolution" is the *unrest of youth*, wiping out a huge number of its best forces.

I have known revolutionaries in Russia who, while perishing themselves, wished to spare the youth. Just recently, one of these individuals, to whom I expressed my views as openly as I do here, asked me to turn to the youth with a comradely admonition; that they should study and prepare for life, not rush into politics prematurely.

The organisers of overseas protests think and feel differently. They are afraid and wish to ensure that I do not have a "cooling" effect on young people. "How many young forces currently forming," they say, "are doomed to moral death, to internal decay in a troubled era, when every [!] evolution [??] of a person who is apparently already established [that is, me, a sinner. - *L.T.*], serves as an encouragement to be hesitant and indecisive, to be a saddlebag".[30]

I deliberately quote these lines. This is a vivid signal of decline, indicating that the time has come for the masters of that which is "progressive" to think again, the time to set about pondering their personality, mind and conscience again. Let readers only consider the narrow, kagalny[31] spirit pervading the reproaches addressed to me.

"Every" evolution frightens the authors of the "outcry"; moral life for them is to be "like us"; criticism, independent choice, constitute "internal decay"; "hesitance and indecision" they would like to supress, caring nothing for anyone's lack of belief, and instead being content with passive obedience and imitation. Better that they say nothing on moral ideals!

---

[30] **(Ed.)** A Russian insult meaning somebody who is inconsistent, who easily changes their views.

[31] **(Ed.)** From the Jewish root for *crowd*, used to designate Jewish self-government in Eastern Europe. Tikhomirov may be using this term to simply refer to a boisterous mob, or to hint at the Jewish backgrounds of many of his fellow revolutionaries.

No, not that I'd even give them my attention! In such a troubled era, so poor in intellectual labours, so morally degraded, an example of a bold search for truth, an example of honestly rejecting a mistake without trepidation in the face of persecution, slander, abuse; this, I think, is precisely what is most needed, this "hesitance and indecision".

To the hesitant and indecisive! You, who had the good fortune of not yet being numb in the passive quest to become "like us", listen to me, one of the few who are not afraid to give you an account of our experience and our sentiments. You can disagree with me, but just pay attention to my "evolution". You will only benefit from doing so. I can offer you only valuable work. If the manifestation of intellectual labour is unprofitable for any programme, if it requires hypnotised minds to serve its party, if it needs the passive conscience of the Old Believer; this proves only the falsity of said programme. Moral death consists precisely in the ossification of conscience, which is alive only when it acts, evaluates and chooses.

My advice to the youth: think, observe, study, do not take anything at a word, do not succumb to loud phrases, do not allow yourself to be frightened by either "great graves"[32] or "saddlebags". Test something twenty times before concluding.

I say this not only because I am sorry to see youth die. Of course, there is that. I am outraged when I hear the reasoning: "let them riot; it's nothing, of course, and nothing serious can ever come from these youths, but at least we'll have a protest".[33]

I will quite readily admit that I prefer to see small, ordinary people, from whom "nothing serious can ever come", live as best they can in happiness, rather than rot somewhere in exile or in a casemate.[34] But this is not my only point of contention. The personal fates of hundreds of young people are here bound up in exceedingly close proximity with the greatest interests of Russia.

---

[32] Reproaching me for undermining their "authority", emigrants pathetically exclaimed:

We need great graves

If there is no greatness alive...

Finally, a frank admission! (*1895 note*).

[33] A genuine expression of instigators.

[34] **(*Ed.*)** A casemate refers to a vaulted chamber in a fortress, that is, a prison.

The educated youth is a strata from which the state and the intellectual life of the country subsequently grow, a precious layer that prepares invaluable blessings for the homeland if it meaningfully readies itself for its future mission, but which can also bring great evil if it should fail in even a single respect. This imposes serious obligations on students to prepare for their future roles in good faith. It is not enough to have good intentions, it is not enough to have a burning passion; you need knowledge, you need skill, and *especially the development of intellectual independence*. Young Russian students should remember that all future "educators", all those capable of guiding our politics or giving direction to popular conscience; all of them will only emerge from the youth. What kind of bankruptcy is being prepared for the country by a generation that, by the time it matures, will not have produced a sufficient number of courageous, strong-willed individuals, always able to chart their own course, who don't give in to first impressions or the influences of political fashion, and even less so to empty phrases through which charlatans everywhere exploit gullible hearts!

Russia is a country with a great past, which offers hope for an even greater future. But it has its drawbacks, an important one being that which relates especially to students: the extreme insignificance of its seriously educated intelligentsia, of those capable of real intellectual labours. The danger of this drawback is obvious, since this stratum imparts to all the works of the country a certain tone, whether in politics, industry, education etc.

The weakness of this "brain of the country" affects the entire mass of the educated stratum in two ways: firstly, in the form of the poor quality of prevailing ideas, widespread in the public sphere and spread, little by little, to the great mass of the people; secondly, in the very manner of thinking, in the ability to think, in the way that ideas are developed, which remains unsatisfactory.

The low quality of the political and social concepts in circulation in Russia stems from the fact that, due to the insignificance of serious intellectual forces, social science has developed no study of our own country and the social phenomena present in it. The previous censorship is also significantly to blame, but its effects should not be exaggerated. The main reason lies in ourselves, in our way of thinking.

Two aspects are characteristic of the Russian way of thinking (I speak here of the *intelligentsia*): the lack of hunger and respect for facts, and, conversely, a boundless trust in theory, in any hypothesis that sanctifies our desires in the slightest degree. This obviously arises from the brain's low aptitude for intense intellectual labour. The brain, which tires too quickly, cannot cope with the myriad facts which surround our life, and imbibes a kind of disgust for them. The hypothesis, on the contrary, pleases it, providing an apparent understanding of phenomena without any tiring stress. Such inclinations are natural in those who have only just begun academic life. However, they need to be identified, understood and corrected. The environment of youth in education should be especially sensitive to this, since it is precisely where the unique thought of a generation emerges.

Our social thought is overflowing with all kinds of biases, hypotheses, theories, each one more comprehensive and ethereal than the last. The education of the mind is only taken so far in general areas, in general considerations, to the extent I fear that it would in fact diminish the ability to think correctly. The "Russian ingenuity" is manifested among the intelligentsia to a lesser degree than among the peasants; practicality doesn't even bear discussing...

In connection with such a development of the mind, how often the moral life of an educated person represents only two extremes! First, the mad fever of a fanatic who permits no scepticism, who sees in discussion only cruelty or cowardice. But alas! Life does what it wills, not according to theory: it ruthlessly buffets the dreamer, and he, having no content in his mind besides logical constructions, begins to feel anger towards life: it seems to him that life unscrupulously deceives. The second phase then arrives; bitter disappointment which sometimes seeks revenge on a life that did not know how to appreciate such a great man. So appears the desperate revolutionary, and so appears the most heartless careerist.

Part V

The fantasist state of mind, common to the entire circle of those with average education, reaches its apotheosis among revolutionaries. Here, the romanticism[35] of worldview reaches its outer limits. Reality is entirely seen through the prism of theory. There exists nothing that would be reflected in its accurate dimensions when passed through this worldview. One could write entire volumes of critical studies about the lack of artistic truth in revolutionary ideas, where the disproportionality of parts and inflated images constitute a general rule. Of course, it's impossible for me to do this, at least here. But there are several viewpoints about which I must say two or three words in order to direct the attention of young people.

Still, when confronted with revolutionary youth, I hear what I myself once said. Many are pushed into politics prematurely by the idea that Russia is on the verge of destruction and could die as early as tomorrow if it is not saved by extraordinary, revolutionary measures. Sometimes this is said not about Russia, but about the community, etc. From the diagnosis, the conclusion follows axiomatically that waiting is criminal, and everyone should go immediately to save the homeland with the weapons they have.

---

[35] The architects of the outcry recall my declaration that "revolutionary thought is always practicable". If they delved into the meaning of words, instead of just being satisfied with the sound, they would have easily seen that the "revolution" I spoke of, that which has been ongoing since the creation of the world, would be better described, in their rebellious terminology, as "evolution" rather than "revolution", and has nothing to do with their "revolutionary methods of action". My dislike of the "myopic gelerters" is, of course, not an argument, and serves only to *demonstrate* how I tried to save the word revolution then, how I did not want to part with it. (*1888 note*).
(*Tr.*) *Gelerter*, from German, describes anyone who has extensive but bookish knowledge, alienated from the practice and the conditions of real life.

However, what could be more fantastical than such a diagnosis? Whatever the situation of Russia or any social phenomenon, one thing is certain: they can neither perish so quickly nor so easily be saved. I believe in the importance of personality in history; I believe in the influence of ideas: destructive or creative, naturally arising from local life or brought in from the outside; they are no less a real force than material conditions. I am an enemy of the theory that everything happens "by itself". But there is also a measure to everything. Why must we adopt this fraudulent mindset, in which we are only able to assess a person as either a complete zero, or if not, someone who

In stepping on the mountains, causes them to crack... [36]

In fact, there is a third option. In society, as elsewhere in nature, there is an eternal interaction of forces, regular and proportional. A person is something in history, but something of only a certain magnitude. He affects society. But in terms of the speed of development or decay of society, there is a limit, determined by the interaction of generations, and this limit will be crossed by neither malevolence nor benevolence. The difference in the transience of life for the individual and society is such that the individual always has time to discuss and study the situation. In terms of a rapid perishing, it can be observed only in that which is already completely rotten and cannot be saved by any means. Therefore, as the French say, *il faut prendre tout au serieux et rien au tragique.* [37] There is no need to get spooked and rush headlong with no direction. Russia can only triumph if the youth vow not to interfere in politics without devoting at least five to six years to completing a course in the subject, and without some familiarity with Russia, its history, its present situation.

Student intervention in politics produces the most harmful consequences in the form of various demonstrations, when almost round the clock, several hundred young, irreplaceable potencies are snatched from the future during penny protests against some trifling "oppression". "Something is better than nothing," the instigators repeat, "if only to avoid stagnation". And such reasoning,

---

[36] **(Ed.)** Said of Alexander Suvarov (1729-1800), a Russian general and one of the most talented commanders in history. Masterminding a host of military victories during the 1700s, he lost not a single major battle.

[37] **(Ed.)** Fr: *Everything should be taken seriously without tragedy.*

unfortunately, acts even today to destroy Russian civilisation in the womb!

I ask, however: is it stagnation when students prepare to serve Russia with the religious trepidation described in the recollections of those circles of the 40s? Is it a moment of stagnation when Belinsky responds with reproach to the invitation to go to lunch: "We have not yet decided whether God exists, and you 'have lunch'"?[38] Is there a state of stagnation when young people genuinely try to understand the history of their country, its institutions, the general laws of social phenomena, when they choose only the best, most suitable means for the future action of everyone and prepare for such things?

On the other hand, are we to see great moral strength, a great development of self-mastery, in this ability to act according to calculations and plans dreamt up in reflective flashes, by which hundreds and thousands of young people, even if triggered by something unpleasant or abnormal, rob Russia of everything of value they might bring to it? Beside an honest impulse, I see here a huge dose of frivolity. I do not here advocate any "statutes", any "administration", but simply ask: is such behaviour most appropriate for a youth worthy of its future civic responsibilities? Should it not aim higher than these insignificant unrests, should it not understand that it has no right to destroy the very force which, in several years, could grow into such a huge asset for Russia?

I have already heard the following objection: "You place impossible demands on young people; they cannot have such restraint and take life so seriously". I do not accept such an objection. The majority of students would be perfectly capable of this *in itself* and would be able to restrain the rest of their fellows if they were not constantly weighed down by the various revolutionary viewpoints. Is it not a fact that if a university fails to have a riot for just eight months, accusations start flying from various "progressives", that "the students have been vulgarised, trampled, corrupted" and who knows what else? Leave aside even that which has the character of direct incitement, such as, for example, arguments that affect young people: "yes, it would be nice to thoroughly prepare and acquire a public

---

[38] **(Ed.)** Refers to a conversation that supposedly unfolded between the Russian literary critic Vissarion Belinsky (1811-1848) and the author Ivan Turgenev (1818-1883).

position. Then one could have a serious, deep influence... But after all, while in the course of such service and finding your way; will you not inevitably *deteriorate*, disappear in the sense of a vital force that wants to act"? I mention this reasoning because it is extremely widespread, and in support of its correctitude one can often hear references to certain *facts*. I myself know such facts; but, at least in my opinion, they are best explained in a completely different way.

A person who refuses to engage in rebellion is all too often regarded as *spoilt*, as self-serving, a rake-fisted careerist. But this is a consequence of those truly perverse ideas, according to which it seems that only by rebelling, by bringing destruction right and left, can a person remain *honest*. This point of view is so rooted in our popular concepts that a person rarely leaves the revolutionary milieu *out of conviction*, and for the most part; *against conviction*, under the pressure of the instincts of a matured organism. The revolutionary who concedes does not know how to understand the truth, does not know how to escape the adopted ideas of rebellion, but only gets the sense that he wants a better life. Pausing, he interprets this as a concession, as a fall. Such a change appears as a fall, and since he falls by abandoning an idea, the absurdities of which he does not yet realise, a person will of course simply wave off everything and sink...

But I do not appeal to weakness, to appetite, to selfishness, but to conscience and reason... When a person believes that his duty is to smash and hurl, I only tell him that this is a mistake, and, if he applies judgment, he often ends up agreeing with me, not in the form of a concession, but a conscious conviction. And then, what *spoiling* can be! A man over the years becomes, of course, calmer, more circumspect; this is inevitable, and there is nothing wrong with it, for every generation finds that prudence is no less necessary than zeal. But it is strange to even have to argue that a more calm and deliberate service to the country does not at all preclude sincerity and honesty. It is enough, finally, to look at the facts. In those cases where a person serves peaceful development not by cowardice, but by conviction, he often shows great virtue. I suspect, rummaging through old memories, each reader will be able to find one or two such examples. If there are still few of them; the fault lies with the theories that prevail in our country, and not with the poor educational value of deliberate activity.

Part VI

The question of cultural activity leads us directly to the question of *autocracy*, which, however, needs to be explained. At present[39], the attitude towards this form of government is almost the defining feature of the revolutionaries. If a person is against "absolutism", he is "one of us", and even the socialists are not particularly interested in the rest of his views. As for cultural activity; it's hardly worth mentioning: "What cultural activity can there be under an unlimited power!"

Unfortunately, I believe in the sincerity of these words, because I myself pronounced them, but now it's doubly embarrassing to remember them. There is no greater evidence of our lack of culture here in Russia, of our poor grasp of the mind's strength, than our inability to independently evaluate the merits of political forms. First, whatever government we may have, it can take away anything that the people want to imagine, but never the possibility of cultural work (assuming the people are capable of it). Secondly, can one forget his own history to such an extent as to exclaim: "What cultural work under absolutism?!" Was Peter[40] not the tsar? An era scarcely matched in speed and breadth of cultural work? Was it not that of Tsarina Catherine II?[41] Was it not under Nicholas I that all of the social ideas with which Russia still lives today developed? Finally, are there many republics that would have made as many transformations over the course of twenty-five years as Russia did under Emperor Alexander II? In the face of all such facts, we have

---

[39] This remained a question in 1888.

[40] **(Ed.)** Peter I (1672-1725): Russian tsar, the first to bear the title of emperor. Due to his imperial victories and westernising reforms which modernised Russian society, he was given the title *'the Great'*.

[41] **(Ed.)** Catherine II (1629-1796): Empress of Russia who oversaw a significant rise in the empire's military and diplomatic strength, as well as great cultural advancement under a regime of *enlightened absolutism*. She was also titled *'the Great'*.

only miserable platitudes with which to respond, such as the claim that all of this happened "contrary to the autocracy".[42]

But even so, is it not all the same, "thanks to" or "contrary to", since rapid progress was possible?

This is how I approach the question of autocratic power. First of all, as a product of Russian history it doesn't require anyone's consent and can be destroyed by no one, for as long as there are tens and tens of millions in the country who, in politics, neither know nor wish to know anything else. It would be impermissible to disregard the historical will of the people, not to mention that a fact which has lasted a great deal of time always has some good reason for its existence. Therefore, every Russian should recognise the power established in Russia and, when considering improvements, should think about how to make them with the autocracy, under the autocracy.

One revolutionary wrote to me that such an action could only do harm, since people like the Kiselyovs and Milyutins[43], by introducing certain improvements, "slow down the destruction of the existing system". I cannot agree with this point of view in any way.

Firstly, in adhering to it, one can reproach not only Kiselyov and Milyutin, but everyone who has contributed to the development of Russia. Do not Pushkin[44], Gogol[45], Tolstoy[46] serve as evidence that the greatest literary progress is compatible with the autocratic monarchy? Are they not therefore harmful? Has the author of *English Lord George*, in this sense, been more useful for Russia?[47] Did not

---

[42] This is exactly the objection I hear from emigrants. (*1895 note*).

[43] **(Ed.)** Dmitry Milyutin (1816-1912): Russian Minister of War between 1861 and 1881, he was responsible for sweeping military reforms which modernised the army.

[44] **(Ed.)** Alexander Pushkin (1799-1837): Russian poet, playwright and novelist considered to be one of the greatest in the country's history.

[45] **(Ed.)** Nikolai Gogol (1809-1852): Russian dramatist, one of the preeminent literary realists.

[46] **(Ed.)** Leo Tolstoy (1828-1910): Russian writer, commonly regarded as one of the greatest in history due to novels such as *War and Peace* and *Anna Karenina*.

[47] **(Ed.)** Refers to *The Tale of the Adventure of the English Lord George and the Brandenburg Margraine of Frederica Louise* (1782) by Russian novelist Matvey Komarov (1730-1812). The book is an example of disposable mass literature.

Muravyov-Amursky[48] give the autocracy the glory of strengthening Russia in the Pacific? As such, isn't the activity of the commissary thieves scuppering all the efforts of our troops more beneficial? Those who reason so forget that the form of government does not define the entire life of the country. Whatever anyone's personal political ideals may be, a duty to the country forces them to seek the greatest benefit from any circumstances it finds itself in.

What would happen if we, repeating: "the worse, the better", allowed ourselves to deliberately deface and spoil the existing governmental mechanism, bringing about its complete disintegration, but at the same time it turned out that the country was capable of no other form? How would we describe the actions we had taken? How would we evaluate their results?

When we talk about this issue, it is necessary to agree on our starting point: what do we want, where do we wish to end up?

There are two concepts of society and two ideals associated with them. All people agree that society should provide financially, as well as for the means of spiritual and physical development, must secure the rights of the people, their, as they say, "freedom". There is no controversy here. But between the views on the type of society there is a gaping void.

Social organism or social amorphism? These are two opposing perspectives. For some, all work, every function of society, is determined and must be determined in a properly organised way, that is, through specially adapted institutions, equipped, of course, with the competence and power necessary for acting. In this way, human progress occurs, and a society develops, the structure of which is constantly becoming more complicated.

To others, it seems as if society moves towards a kind of simplification, towards a uniform distribution of all duties and all forms of power among the mass of citizens. The functions of institutions are transferred to individuals, and each person comprises a certain fraction of all social competencies.

I am a man after the first concept, and for me, society conceived as an organic process which creates something whole, with growing complexity in its organisation, is not simply an ideal but a fact. I can

---

[48] **(Ed.)** Nikolay Muravyov-Amursky (1809-1881): Russian general and statesman who advanced the empire's territorial conquests in the Far East.

build my social ideals only in accordance with this fundamental, sociological fact.

Returning to the previous argument, I first note that any change in the organisation of central authority can be desirable only when one, the worst, is replaced (and replaced in a real sense, not in that of mere verbiage) with something better. Destruction, which creates nothing, I consider harmful, since it only weakens the social organism.

What will the critics of the political foundations of the Russian system replace it with? First of all, the enemies of our system only have the power to disturb it, to interfere with its proper administration and functions. In consisting of this alone, their critical posture is entirely sterile. If we imagine that some emperor agreed or was forced to limit his autocracy for a minute, this restriction would be purely fictitious, since the vast majority of the people would always be ready, at the first word of the tsar, to expel those who were supposedly doing the "limiting"[49]; therefore, the power of the sovereign would, in essence, be limited only by his own acquiescence. What can be achieved by such a "limitation"?

I will, however, say more. If any changes in our system of government were possible, we would do well to consider them with the utmost caution. Every country needs, above all else, a strong government, that is, a government which is not afraid for its existence and is capable of enacting its policies. Moreover, Russia has an extraordinary need for strong government, due to its far-from-complete national tasks and myriad domestic issues that remain unresolved. We need a strong monarchical power, and, when contemplating any improvements, we must firstly be sure that we do not damage the essential merits of our system. Many of us dream of parliamentarism, but there is only one valuable contribution of a parliament; the constant discovery[50] of people's desires and opinions,

---

[49] **(Ed.)** Tikhomirov alludes here to real history. In 1730, having taken the throne under a set of restrictive conditions promulgated by an elite *supreme privy council*, Empress Anna (1693-1740) was petitioned by a populist faction to repudiate the council and strip its members of power, which she did.

[50] The way I expressed this was inaccurate and does not put across what I wished to say in 1888. *Every* assembly of people taken from different walks of life reveals the opinions and desires of the people, but the parliament does it *most poorly*. Parliamentarism, as a system of government, also eliminates that which is usefully provided by a system of assembly. (*1895 note*).

and parliamentarism, in fact, as a system of state administration, is highly unsatisfactory.

The third observation I must make is that every government, unless it finds action impossible, acts approximately in that direction determined by the material conditions of the country and the ideas that appeal to it. This is where one must look for a real source of the many disorders in Russia.

With any form of government, from where can personages and events arise, if not from among the educated class? The most capable and well-meaning ruler can only successfully or unsuccessfully *appoint people*, but he cannot personally solve all the issues of administration, sociology and political economy. If the stratum of those representing the concentrated wisdom of the country is filled with frivolous, chaotic, or theoretically inapplicable ideas; who is to blame?

When we look at the *political* role played by our educated class throughout the nineteenth century, and especially in our time, it far from always deserves a certificate of maturity and has often only served to deprive the government of the opportunity to use the country's educated forces. I'm ignoring the exceptions here. As a general rule, young people, and, for the most part, the most progressive part of society, live with their heads in the clouds, and in practice they throw themselves into anything that will bring despair to the state: this is why you see Russians participating in the Polish rebellion[51], joining those with dreams of a *federation of independent communities* and plans for widespread uprisings, or crafting the ideas and practice of the *terrorist struggle*. All this is done with the conviction of a fanatic, with passionate energy; even an outburst! What are the moderates and the older generation doing at this time? As a rule, they demonstrate a complete inability to work independently and cannot create anything capable of disciplining the minds of the youth, of subordinating them to the influence of any serious, scientifically developed doctrines. Secondly, these older generations are so timid that they are actually afraid to contradict the progressives, and sometimes directly fall under their influence. In

---

[51] **(Ed.)** Refers to the January Uprising of 1863, an insurrection in the Polish lands that had as its aim the reconstitution of the Polish-Lithuanian Commonwealth. The Polish conscripts who started the doomed rebellion were joined by many left-wing Russians.

short; this more moderate stratum is generally completely unable to control the orientation of the mind and give it direction. Meanwhile, while it does not even dream of limiting the supreme power, it does behave with such little tact that it arouses suspicion and mistrust in this regard. Lacking the power to create or maintain a constitution, they constantly bother the government with complaints about the "crowning of the building"[52], and, in order to prove the need for this crowning, they resort to the most tendentious, biased criticism of all government measures, regardless of their nature. This causes understandable displeasure and further aggravates mutual relations.

Under such conditions, progressive elements, one might say, exclude themselves from participation in the governing of the country. Insofar as they do participate, it is only thanks to the personal work ethic of the liberals, which is often as strong as their partisan discernments are weak. Who can be blamed for the fact that the government was forced to take on people, and with them systems, where this could be done without fear for the integrity of the throne, for example, in the case of Katkov?[53]

But Katkov, who, as a practical politician possessed extraordinary insight and independence of thought, something distinguished in Russia, was far from a creative mind when it came to social problems.[54]

Frightened by the intensity of the revolutionary movement and the powerlessness of the liberals, standing watch at his post, "against the current" for a whole century, he put great care into developing the purely external power of the government. In terms of creation, he did nothing, and if he prevented the government from making several mistakes, he also suggested others.[55]

---

[52] (**Ed.**) *Crowning the building* was a euphemism among Russian liberals to refer to the institution of a permanent, elected assembly in Russia.

[53] (**Ed.**) Mikhail Katkov, see p.xv.

[54] I must now add a reservation that, having better studied the journalistic activities of Katkov, I have come to a much more positive verdict on the social creativity of his mind. He *understood* surprisingly much, but his practical instinct allowed him to understand that in modern Russia he would not have much impact. He did only the bulk of what he could at this time, with faith that the rest would be completed in the future. (*1895 note*).

[55] And here I was unfair to Katkov. However, I'm not rewriting what I did in 1888, confining myself to the reservation that, at that time, I was unaware of many of

The shortcomings of the systems adopted by the government can be blamed primarily on the educated class, both its conservative part, and especially its progressive elements. Let these elements work to develop their own plans, with their own minds, but let these plans be more consistent with the real life of the country; and they will of course receive the same agreement from us as would any such form of government.

This is my opinion.

Katkov's *activities*, hence why I did not properly evaluate his great merits. (*1895 note*).

Part VII

With these sentences I could finish my explanation, since the presentation of my, so to speak, programme, is not among my goals here. But in order to definitively determine my denial of revolutionary ideas, I want to outline in two or three words at least some aspects of that orientation, the triumph of which I would like to see in Russia.

The revolutionary movement is not a cause, but only a symptom of an evil, from which contemporary Russia is the main sufferer. This evil, as I said, is the lack of seriously developed minds among our educated class, as a result of which all the intellectual work of this class is of very low quality. The ensuing collection of flaws that are created by *semi-education*[56] can often be found even within the work of our most outstanding talents. This is the evil that destroys the best aspects of the Russian nature, which once helped our ancestors to create a great country, the country which today we destabilise to the best of our abilities.

The fight against this evil is, in my opinion, the most important task of the present. The fate of Russia essentially depends on whether it can finally develop a core of mature minds strong enough to discipline the rest of the educated class and outline with *its own* works, its own thought and research, the cardinal points of Russia's foundations.

To do this, we need, first of all, a strong shaking up of minds, we need a general reappraisal of our social and political views.

Saying this, I would of course not think of turning to the youth. Such a task is beyond them. It is necessary to turn to the older, upper strata, who must comprehend the righteousness of the ideas I have

---

[56] The evil of semi-education is not to be found in a small amount of knowledge (the peasant has even less), but in the manner of assimilating knowledge only slightly, and from other people's words, in the habit of being satisfied with half-knowledge, etc., generally, in the poor discipline of the mind.

expressed. It is their responsibility to chart a new course. The obligation to do something to puzzle out a positive and constructive worldview lies especially with my peers, who, like me, were enthralled by so many "revolutions", having experienced and pondered much. Their experience and age have, of course, taught them a great deal and aroused in them the desire for sobriety of thought.[57]

The same responsibilities lie also with another part of our generation, people who were at one time sceptical enough not to be captivated by the "movement", and have now become full-fledged, often honourable, members of Russian society. The means of the peaceful development of the country are in their hands. Finally, there are the many pioneers who have long paved the way for what I speak of, but who acted alone and did not boldly raise their heads to declare that they are the real salt protecting the country from putrefaction, the country torn by the struggle of revolutionaries and reactionaries.

The development of Russian thought, of Russian science, especially in the areas where it lacks the most; the social and political, the study of the country, the updating of Russian education, the development and regularisation of the press; these constitute the main tasks. Next to them is the development of labour *productivity*, technology, improved forms of labour, etc. Lastly come improvements in the organisation of different segments of the population, chief among which will consist of imparting a serious and strictly practical character to local self-government. I won't dwell here on sketching the outline of this enormous task. I note only one circumstance.

Of course, for the correct course of cultural development to take root in the country, promotion through government measures is necessary. It is impossible, for example, to hope that, given the weakness of our cultural development, student unrest will cease without normalising the situation of student life. In suppressing the riots and the interference of youth in political activities beyond their competence, the government should, however, satisfy the legitimate needs of the youth, just as in Germany, France, etc. It is necessary that young people be permitted to study, to reason, and it is necessary that they live fuller lives with more leisure, etc. Without appropriate

---

[57] Alas! Vain hope, apparently... (*1895 note*).

government measures or, at least, without the greatest caution in choosing trustees and inspectors, the efforts of the most well-meaning people will be smashed against the disgruntled mindset of the students. Similarly, lack of freedom of scientific research hinders the maturation of Russian thought. Of course, complaints about censorship are extremely exaggerated and, in the main, the work of the Russian mind always finds the opportunity to manifest itself in our literature. However, Russian science is still so weak that even the slightest hindrance to its development would undoubtedly be harmful.[58]

The elimination of these obstacles could be achieved imperiously by the government. In the same way, it could deal with the zemstvo.[59] Its current organisation is clearly unsatisfactory and inevitably sets it on a collision course with the administration. The merger of the zemstvo with the administration, that is, the expansion of the latter's scope of jurisdiction, and the subordination of the former to necessary regulation and responsibilities, generally giving it the value of a certain organ of the government, would eliminate many misunderstandings and many sources of discontent.[60]

How would this even be done without government intervention? Thus, the question which takes the stage, so to speak, is political: what can we do with it?

I'm close to finishing now, and I want to say a few words. In this regard, we are real *faiseurs d'embarras*[61] and we create fears and obstacles for ourselves. Everywhere, in all countries, under all forms

---

[58] I repeat this now, although I know better than I did then how many of our certified "scientists" use "freedom" only for biting publicistic articles. I cannot but add, however, that the freedom of scientific research in our country is constrained mainly not by censorship, but by the extremely despotic "public opinion" of the liberal stratum, devoid of even a spark of respect for the work of human thought, crowning with laurels any distortion of science so long as it has a partisan slant, and contrariwise pushing back hard on every word that goes beyond the framework of partisan "truth". It is sometimes a pity and a shame to look at *this* slavish state of our professors. Only public opinion itself can eliminate *these* obstacles. (*1895 note*).

[59] (*Ed.*) See p.xii.

[60] As you know, the government has taken this path. Remarkable is the underdevelopment of our "liberals," who have crossed swords with the government precisely over this most important reform. (*1895 note*).

[61] (*Ed.*) Fr: *Creators of difficulties*.

of government, the task of informing the central authority, in a timely manner, of the country's needs and encouraging it to accept necessary reforms is one of the most difficult. I recall, however, that in our history we have several brilliant eras of reform. If, in the current situation of Russia, according to its citizens, there really is a place for serious reforms; they must be sought as they are in any other country, that is, in accordance with the existing legal means of political action.

The source of legislative and executive power (according to Russian law) is the sovereign of the country. In republican countries, this source is voters. In both cases, political action, no matter where it emerges from, manifests itself only through established institutions. These institutions in Russia present no less ways to operate than in another country. We have the Council of State, the Senate, ministries with various additional bodies and several perpetual commissions. Not to mention social activities of an informal nature, such as journalism, work through various scientific societies, etc. The party of legal progress seems to have a very wide field of action. Let her people serve, work, let them always have a yearly proposal adapted to the needs of the situation, the practicality of which can be proved to the sovereign. At the moment when the emperor decides to call to power a progressive party (which he will certainly do from time to time, once he is convinced that this party sincerely recognises his sovereign rights), the progressive party should be ready to justify this call and to do only what is possible given the conditions of Russia. Have we not, unfortunately, witnessed how those called to power found themselves, despite their all-Russian reputation, completely without a proposed system and themselves did not know what to do? I do not here seek to blame anyone individually when everyone is to blame, but I only note the fact which should not have been. Ministries do not exist to teach political literacy, but to meet the needs of the country. One must prepare for things in advance. And then, if the supreme power (for whatever reason) considers it more advantageous to turn instead to others, what is one to do? It remains only to submit to this decision and take advantage of the time in freedom from power to seriously prepare for the next opportunity. Is this not what Gladstone[62] does,

---

[62] (*Ed.*) William Gladstone (1809-1898): British liberal politician who served as prime minister on four occasions between 1868 and 1894.

having lost a majority in the chamber? For any centre of power, there are moments of forward movement, moments of stagnation, moments of reaction. There is nothing here which should cause anyone to lose heart or feel indignation, but instead, you should work, making it a rule to look for the reasons for your failure, first in yourself, and only then in others.[63]

---

[63] It is clear that I did not mean by our "progressive party" our banal liberals, but that stratum of emissaries of "development" whom I had only expected to appear. In recent years, they, while barely noticeable, have become much more numerous, and due to this, the foregoing considerations gain greater significance in my eyes. (*1895 note*).

Appendix No. 1

Such was the content of my pamphlet, which I reprint word for word, with the exception of a few places that required, as I explained above, changes.

It had, in addition, two appendices that would be incomprehensible to readers without major additions. The long and short of it is this. The emigrants, led by Lavrov[64], trying to protect their herd from my "harmful" influence, tried their best to *personally* undermine me. An old, commonplace tactic that I subsequently encountered in Russia upon my return. However, it was difficult to put forward anything against me, a man who enjoyed almost the most impeccable reputation in their midst. Therefore, the émigré gentlemen resorted to various dark insinuations about the alleged *suddenness* of my change in views. It was a completely conscious lie on their part. Other external critics might not have known of my turning point and even my previous views in their actual fullness. But to the emigrants themselves, especially Lavrov and his closest friends, my increasingly firm renunciation of the revolution was so well known that they had been trying for a long time to block young people from even visiting me. To say directly that I was no longer their man was disadvantageous for them, of course, because, with the possible exception of Lavrov himself, there was not a single person whom the "radical" youth believed more than me. My renunciation of the revolution could lead to similar renunciations on the part of many others. Therefore, Lavrov & Co., while continuing to present me as one of "theirs", only said that I was a sick man, that I needed peace of mind, that I valued my privacy and did not like visitors. At that time, I lived far from Paris, in a remote area, and really did not like to see emigrants, since I was immersed in my studies and thoughts. And my health was indeed greatly shaken. But I always welcomed *Russians* from Russia, happily and consistently dissuaded

---

[64] **(Ed.)** Peter Lavrov, see p.x.

them from participating in the revolution and advised many emigrants to submit petitions for their return to the homeland. Having heard my reasoning, for a long time already my Russian interlocutors remarked with surprise: "Yes, he is an ardent monarchist". It would thus be difficult to talk about the "suddenness" of my change in views. As such, Lavrov was not ashamed to resort to juggling "documents". He specifically referred, as proof of my supposedly recent, fiercely revolutionary mood in 1886, to one of my "letters" to him and to an article of "mine" in a foreign magazine... In reality, the "letter" was not a letter at all, but a cursory note of five or six lines, containing in no sense an expression of my views, but instead simply a rebuke to the rattlepates of "revolution" who did not even read their own party publications. Of course, five or six lines, jotted down quickly and not intended for the public but for a person who understands your point perfectly, can always be subjected, if desired, to an unfair interpretation. This is what Lavrov did. Even more remarkable is his reference to "my" article. In fact, it was written by *Lavrov himself... I only* read it in print. My only fault here was that I relied on Lavrov's good faith. Here is what happened. The last issue of the publication, on which I collaborated with Lavrov, slowed down production due to a scandalous incident[65], which is inconvenient to explain in detail here. Of course, it was necessary to inform the readers. Lavrov pestered me about this to such an extent that *I* agreed to do it. I said that it doesn't matter who writes, but the crafty old man insistently asked me to do it, under the pretext that, after all, I was a member of the enterprise. Meanwhile, in my home life, where various illnesses had taken hold, there was such chaos that I was not at all up to the task of writing. Yet, it needed to be written *immediately*. Lavrov suggested that he would write a few lines himself, in my name. It was embarrassing for me to refuse and in so doing betray a clear distrust of the old man, and indeed, in all truthfulness, what was there not to trust? A few lines of the actual statement seemed to pose no risk, and I agreed so as not to delay the liquidation of the publication, an event which broke the last strands of my involuntary ties with revolutionary "figures". However, I still felt uneasy. I genuinely did not expect dishonesty in this matter, but "for the sake of fidelity", I nevertheless took a moment out of my day, and no more

---

[65] **(Ed.)** The incident referred to here was the trashing of the Bulletin's printworks in Switzerland by agents of the Russian state.

than a few hours later sent *my own* little statement. It turned out, however, that I was too late. Lavrov, with the greatest haste, scribbled a fierce little article *for me* and immediately handed it over to the printer... Everyone in that circle was aware of how dissatisfied I was with this, and how I lambasted the not only furious but asinine note when I read it in print. So, Lavrov *referred to his own article*, written under my name, the content of which remained unknown to me even in 1888, to characterise *my* views in 1886!

In the appendices to the pamphlet, my goal was to expose such dishonest methods of argumentation and to appeal to Lavrov & Co. to behave more decently. I must say, however, that casting my "pearls" proved complete useless. It was, in part, a result of my naïveté. But then, I was in a special, idealistic mood. Emerging from a brutal internal withdrawal, exhausted but, so to speak, a victor over myself, I had great optimism about others. It seemed to me impossible not to awake people with the honesty of thought and conscience! After all, people are people. Why would they be worse than me? Of course, I did not awake anything in anyone, and I say this not to pass condemnation. A person is awakened not by the words and exhortations of others, but by his inner development, and, until it has occurred, the words of others are fruitless, just as they would have been fruitless for me a few years before.

These words of mine are good only as an aid to those who have already begun the internal process of awakening. There were too few of such people in 1888, but there are many more now, in 1895. For them, I think, my explanations which trace the course of my internal schism, may turn out to be useful material, an acquaintance with which will help them understand themselves.

Appendix No. 2: A Few Comments on the Debate Among the Emigrants

For almost a whole year now, I have been the subject of fierce polemics by Russian emigrants in Paris and Switzerland. I would not have thought to bring an exposition on this subject within the borders of the homeland, had it not already preceded me, sans my own input. Moreover, the desire of emigrants to destroy me has the goal of manipulating the strata of youth that are still subject, unfortunately, to their influence. Some explanation is necessary on my part.

I mainly direct this explanation to the Russian youth, even to those "comrades in Russia" to whom Mr. Lavrov writes his "letter" about me. I do not appeal to my émigré opponents due to an absence of "common ground" in the sense of ideas or desires, which likewise explains why Mr. Lavrov does not contend with me directly ("Letter to Comrades in Russia," pp.2-3). Such considerations were relevant when it came to the scribes and Pharisees, the inquisitors, etc. For me, in the determination of truth, neither Jew nor Greek exists. I believe that two human beings can always find *common ground* in the form of the truth of factual, moral and universal interests. The only condition necessary for this is conscientiousness, sincerity, and a commitment to argue honestly. Thus, I did not hesitate to call upon the reason and conscience of emigrants and revolutionaries in my pamphlet *Why I Ceased to Be a Revolutionary*.

Unfortunately, my opponents refused to argue in good faith. They chose a different approach. They endeavoured to isolate me, to ensure that others neither listen to nor read me. To this end, they put to work all their "party discipline". In polemics, they relied on the dissemination of fabrications and slander that went beyond the limits of what I could imagine.

According to a certain Svetlov[66] (*Cri du Peuple*, August 21), I just sold out, seduced by Katkov's laurels and roubles; he calls me *traotre*[67], adding: *qui dit traotre dit policier*[68]; he expresses fear that I might inform against him.

G. Serebryakov[69], who only recently told me: "You are too modest! You yourself know that you are the only person with anything new to say", now relates to his readers an alleged history of my development, which demonstrates that I was always insignificant, led by great comrades, and that I fell so suddenly due to fear of the government, as soon as there was no longer a clear leadership (*An Open Letter to Lev Tikhomirov*, pp.2-3).

P. Lavrov is not far behind his young friends. He is not ashamed to compare me with Degayev[70], obscuring, as usual, the meaning he intends to convey, but all the more so throwing in the seed of slander, which ought to grow magnificently in the soil of the inflamed minds he has cultivated. He has no shame in stating: "L.A. Tikhomirov is a *stranger*," something he repeats several times, with the bitterness of a medieval rabbi, emphasising the word *stranger*. He finds legitimate the indignation of those "who are too indignant to even think about what justice dictates" (p.31). I therefore "must expect all the consequences of my *act*". He calls for retaliatory measures: "If every supporter of the socialist cause was sure that his comrades would not forgive him a single act harmful to the success of the party... he would, in many cases, decide against such action" (p.3). And, after all this anathematisation, P. Lavrov declares everything to be my fault, as if I had moved from the camp of the *persecuted* to that of the *persecutor* (p.31). This is me; slandered, given over to the deluge, to retribution, but I find myself among the persecutors of Mr. Lavrov and his comrades!

---

[66] (**Ed.**) *Svetlov* appears to have been the pseudonym of one Valerii Ivchenko, an obscure revolutionary exile. *Cri du Peuple* (Cry of the People) was one of France's leading socialist papers.

[67] (**Ed.**) Fr: *Traitor*.

[68] (**Ed.**) Fr: *Who says "traitor" says "police agent"*.

[69] (**Ed.**) It is unclear who this refers to, however the most likely candidate would be Esper Serebryakov (1854-1921), a Russian émigré who published the left-wing newspaper *Nakanune* (On the Eve).

[70] (**Ed.**) Sergey Degayev, see p.xi.

Situating a polemic on such solid ground that, in fact, there's nothing to "argue with" (pp.2-4), and you must cast about for a weapon to wield against me (p.8), my opponents are not shy about manufacturing them. Either ambiguous *petits papiers*[71], or some anonymous "comrades" (perhaps those I turned away at the doorstep) who testify that they did not notice any internal struggle in me. "Witnesses" against me, like Mr. Serebryakov mentioned above, expose all manner of "inaccuracies" in my testimony.

One, for example, writes in the pamphlet *Revolution or Evolution*[72] that he is struck by the unexpectedness of my radically new assessment of terrorism and revolution; he protests against me and exposes me. Yet, this same man, a year before, collaborated with me in planning the programme of a failed magazine. The programme was based on the consideration that in Russian political thought there exists no idea unique enough in breadth and *positivity*; the development of this *healthy* worldview was the task of the magazine, which declared itself to be *outside the parties*. A peaceful resolution to the various difficulties of the present was recognised as not only *desirable*, but also *possible*. Terrorism was defined as "a painful and even very dangerous phenomenon," among other things, because it distorts ideas. This same person, who reads this with the *personal* knowledge that it was I who used all my efforts to give this magazine a purely cultural character and to expel the revolutionary point of view from the programme, he now protests against the "surprise", as if he really knows nothing. Is there even a glimmer of conscience in such false witnesses?

In the same way, Lavrov quotes one of my notes, supposedly proving my revolutionary zeal, while I spoke so frankly with the individual mentioned in the note that he described me everywhere as a *monarchist*.

In exactly the same way, in the 'Bulletin of the 'People's Will'', as evidence of this zeal, Lavrov refers to a statement written not by me, but by Lavrov himself and not even read by me; a fact known to all in our circle.

I mention all these squabbles only in order to show readers the impossibility of contending (other than in a formal court) with such

---

[71] **(Ed.)** Fr: *Small pieces of paper.*
[72] **(Ed.)** See p.xiv.

polemicists and "witnesses". The point is not the absence of a common ideological ground, but the fact that gentlemen émigrés have liberated themselves from all "fetters" of good faith.

But I must explain myself to the readers.

What is the true reason the émigré gentlemen are so indignant against me? It is not a thankless task to ponder their state of mind. It represents a good example of naïve conceit combined with extreme smallness of thought.

The revolutionaries are sincerely convinced that they march at the head of historical progress. According to their concepts, the development of man brings him closer to them, while his regression extends this distance. There is a huge difference between Mr. Tikhomirov, Lavrov, and those "working for peaceful progress" in Russia. They cannot be treated equally. "Some of them [workers for peaceful progress. - *L.T.*] may join our ranks tomorrow," he explains, "and we will accept them with joy [what an honour! - *L.T.*]. Their mistake is that they have not gone far enough, but they have not retreated; nothing prevents them from going further [still! - *L.T.*]. The position of L. A. Tikhomirov is entirely different. *He saw and turned away*. He was at the front and retreated" (p.31).

This is the heart of the matter and constitutes my crime. The historical outlook presented by my opponent is common to the entire revolutionary world. Not only Mr. Lavrov, but even the very first self-taught anarchists, somehow educated with pamphlets, are just as convinced they have some kind of "science", freedom, progress etc. on their side.

But, in contrast to this, I affirm precisely that there is nothing more fanciful than such claims. In fact, the revolutionary worldview is a conclusion drawn from the most insignificant number of facts, and, moreover, facts incorrectly interpreted. This applies as perfectly to P. Lavrov as it does to Mssrs. Serebryakov and Simonovsky[73] & Co., because he uses no more facts to substantiate his opinions than they do; any knowledge he has besides exists in mechanical theories or not at all. Hence, all their argumentation is equally banal and superficial.

I used to think using the same system as Mr. Lavrov, that is, I discarded most of what I saw, what I read. My "act", in essence,

---

[73] **(Ed.)** An unidentified émigré.

consisted only in the fact that I finally decided to see what I was looking at, and at that point, "breaking away" was inevitable.

My critic rightly says, I saw and turned away. Without a doubt! And who would not turn away when they saw?

I, he reproaches, "was at the front and retreated". Of course, not knowing what was being done "at the front," I, like many others, might have lived by a simple *trust* in such people, and in doing so I would never have allowed myself to think, and thus, could have remained forever under the sway of "progressive ideas". But, seeing the facts and not fearing the conclusions which followed, I could not help but "back off". Since beginning to think, I could not avoid admitting to myself that "revolutionary practice" is all too often criminal, sometimes to a terrifying degree, and that theories are always juvenile, sketchy and sometimes absolutely ludicrous.

Emerging from beneath the influence of schemas and clichés, I could not help but see that my retreat from the "revolution" was not only not a retreat from freedom and development, but quite the opposite. Mssr. Lavrov doesn't actually go "forward" at all, and rather than guiding humanity, he simply wanders *along both* verges of the road, treading around in the same place for decades, and sometimes traveling backwards in relation to the rest of humanity. These people do not lead history but are the by-product of a historical course of development which casts aside useless elements left and right. The real, living power of history lies precisely in those "peaceful workers", *with we* who are treated with such dismissive indulgence by Lavrov and his ilk.

I say "with we" because this is not the case for everybody. I wish I could witness a revolutionary telling Taine[74] or Pasteur[75] that *nothing prevents* them from joining the "party"! He would probably hear in reply: "Dear friend, believe that it's more difficult for us to become revolutionaries than for you to cease being so, since it's impossible for us to descend to a lower, less mature stage of worldview; if it's difficult for you to maintain such a worldview, it may be possible to ascend to our level". It's characteristic that Lavrov obviously does not understand this and claims with all seriousness

---

[74] **(Ed.)** Hippolyte Taine (1828-1893): French historian notable for applying a naturalist outlook to the sociological analysis of history.

[75] **(Ed.)** Louis Pasteur (1822-1895): French biologist famed for discovering the principle of vaccination and often referred to as the father of germ theory.

that my accusation of unreality directed at the revolutionary worldview is *unfounded*. What a marvel! I would understand if Lavrov began to uphold the importance of unconscious historical movements, while still failing to grasp the fantastical nature of revolutionary ideas and assessments; this is truly incredible…

But whether Lavrov finds it difficult to assimilate new perspectives, alien to his generation, he still has no right to resort to ignominious methods of combatting me. A thinking man must understand that other generations have the right to think, and the trend of throwing mud at them for this is inexcusable. In each generation, this is not done by its best representatives.

Regardless, let us return to the claims of the revolutionaries to pose as the vanguard of mankind. Are these people really *ahead*? Following them, will we arrive at a *higher* state? I would hope that to go forward means to develop strength, to improve moral and intellectual life, and to implement justice… Do Lavrov and his comrades show us the way to such things? I cannot think so.

In moral terms, I immediately find that Lavrov's ideas lead directly to a certain revival of extremely primitive, imperfect forms of morality. Instead of a brotherhood of universal humanity and supreme justice reigning over all private (including group) interests, Lavrov resurrects the Old Testament form of group solidarity. Axiomatically, close relationships develop within the group (or party), but the outside, so to speak, external world, is just a collection of goys, infidels, something like a concept of *hosts, Germans*, mutes[76], with whom the Lavrovs of the world cannot even converse (they share no common language). Undoubtedly, they intend to "save" this external world, but, firstly, in the herd, in all humanity, individuals who fit the rubric of "enemies of socialism" have no right to even expect justice. In relation to them, as can be seen from the foregoing, the revolutionaries allow themselves to forget even what honour demands. Secondly, when it comes to "salvation" for the external world, neither sincerity nor respect is shown.

I recall Lavrov's last tract on *the role and forms of socialist propaganda*. If he expresses his idea clearly, without the usual

---

[76] **(Ed.)** A range of synonyms to describe outsiders. Goy is a derogatory word to describe non-Jews. All Europeans in Russia were sometimes collectively described as German. Mutes was another nickname for these Europeans who could not speak Russian.

omissions, he teaches (p.5), in essence, the following system: set the "petty bourgeoise" against the "industrial tycoon" and the worker against the "employer", that is, against the very same petty bourgeoise. The cosmopolitan socialist is even encouraged to rely on patriotism if this is beneficial (for the "cause"). "Whether the propagandist makes use of the term "socialism" in all these cases or not, it makes no difference," the wise teacher adds. "All that matters is that ideas develop in minds which undermine faith in the inviolability of the existing order of things, and indicate the path of struggle against this order" (p.6). Of course, the young adherent of "socialist morality" will apply these resplendent rules to "instigating riots" and "terrorist actions", because neither one nor the other, according to Lavrov, runs contrary to socialist propaganda, and one need only take into consideration "who has cause to act, bringing about revolt, striking the imagination of society with terroristic deeds" (p.10). In all this, the question of *justice* is not even raised. Lavrov teaches us to think only of *expediency* from the point of view of the implementation of his idea. The thoroughbred spirit of Jesuitism[77] emerges through all this propaganda, in which there is absolutely no respect for the thought, conscience and freedom of others, whether they are individuals or even a hundred million people united by a single faith, an idea.

In demonstrating the criminality of terrorism in my pamphlet, I said that all should recognise the forms of power established by the people and that, in forcibly overthrowing them, we commit a tyrannical act. To this, Lavrov objects that it is only necessary to recognise the *true* (emphasised by him) interests of the people, and not at all those which are simply "familiar forms of thought and life, even for millions". Faced with the people, "whose sad history has not allowed them to develop properly", the revolutionary should not "yield" (p.10). And if all that was discussed here was the freedom to propagandise, then I spoke nothing of it, and only raised my voice against *violent* actions. It is in defence of these that Lavrov speaks. But how does one know what constitutes a *true* need of the people, and what does not? This is again to be determined not by the people, but by the revolutionaries themselves. Then, if the people refuse to

---

[77] **(Ed.)** For a strong treatment of this Jesuitical morality, see Ilyin, I. (2018). *On Resistance to Evil by Force.* Zvolen: Taxiarch Press, pp.175-188.

recognise the justice of their determinations, the worse for them: they will be forced, strong-armed; all that they hold sacred will be destroyed by dagger and dynamite. The "progressive" kagal can allow itself whatever it wants, because one rule applies for the "enlightened", and another for the "aliens", the uncircumcised…

To what extent such a dual "morality" is beneficial from a tactical point of view does not concern me, but as a moral doctrine, such "progressive" ideas obviously carry us thousands of years backwards, to pre-Christian times. There is also no doubt that with such a common morality based on contempt for the rights of others, it is impossible to be truly moral even within one's circle, no matter how seemingly united and materially in solidarity it is. It is enough to observe to what extent freedom of conscience is disallowed here and what kind of strict discipline, what supervision of the circle's members Lavrov himself requires. "The ways in which a socialist earns his daily bread," he says, "his friendships and personal acquaintances, his *intimate family life* [?]; he cannot say about these things that they are his business and nobody else's" (p.17). Comrades must monitor everything from the street to the bedroom and strictly suppress all deviations from what is prescribed.

All this is not only unscrupulous, but also very archaic, backward in the extreme relative to the already quite distant era when Christianity, sanctifying the power of public authority, thereby sanctified the spiritual autonomy of the individual, which Lavrov seeks to simultaneously destroy. Such a teaching cannot lead us forward! In order not to notice this, one must be very downtrodden and coarse.

As regards intellectual content, it is again difficult to recognise the pretensions of Lavrov and his comrades. Rereading their writings, one involuntarily recalls the merchant Gleb Uspensky's[78] words at the Old Believers cathedral: "God forbid! Whatever words are spoken, not a one is less than two hundred years old". I remember their "progressive" words from school. And it's hardly surprising, because what kind of intellectual work can be done when everything is already known, decided, when there is nothing to think about, and one is not permitted to think? Just as the moral requirements of justice

---

[78] **(Ed.)** Gleb Uspensky (1843-1902): A prominent Russian liberal publicist, key to the Narodnik movement mentioned on p.ii.

are erased in the "progressive" stratum before the "interests of the party", so too the development of thought and creativity is swept before them so as not to shake the foundations of party propaganda. The interests of "revolutionary action" devour everything, and conscience and thought are equally deprived of all freedom.

What is this new progress? All of it has been practiced from time immemorial with the difference that the authorities are usually much more tolerant, and that familiar censorship is understandable on the part of the state, since the goal of the state is not so much the development of the future as the maintenance of public life in the present, which implies the need for a certain amount of custodianship and repression. But censorship (merciless censorship at that) in a party that claims to recreate the world on the basis of all kinds of freedoms; this is a contradiction and belies a level of sophistry and insincerity in the critiques, polemics and thought of the "party". People cry out against censorship while they themselves are true inquisitors. I am a living example of the immensity, in this milieu, of the inclination to destroy everything that breaks rank. If Mssrs. Lavrov[79] and those around him are trying to crush even me with suspicions, false accusations, abuse, etc., then what do they do with those who are weaker, whom they can really intimidate daily, every minute, as regards all matters of thought and life? With such a system of mutual dullness, minds inevitably become cowardly and dishonest. People shout about thought, development, yet they respect nobody; they shout against *persecution*, and they themselves browbeat with all the strength they have; they shout against violence, and they themselves kill, and moreover, they want to force entire nations to live like this or not at all... Where is the "forward" in all this, where is the light of progress? Is a state of mind which combines such glaring contradictions a state of *higher* development? Is this type of mind not lower than what is already now considered among us ordinary, unenlightened people as a developed mind?

But what about, they will say, the ideas themselves, for the triumph of which the revolutionaries lower their conscience and mind, can these ideas themselves be lofty? We should remember, that in order to implement these ideas, Mssrs. Lavrov must first

---

[79] **(Ed.)** In using the plural Mssrs. here, Tikhomirov is using Lavrov as the personification of all his critics in the diaspora.

indoctrinate at least a significant minority of mankind, that is, among the mass of people abroad and at home, to cease the work of thought and conscience. A new order would be good! Ideas developed *through* the practice we witness on the *"frontline"*, will perforce not lead *forward*, but far *backward*.

To briefly demonstrate this, let Lavrov cast a glance at his own camp for once. In the present case, the emigrants have gathered all their strength to nullify my "harmful" influence. What have they proved? What have they refuted? I have described in detail the degrading effect of terrorism, and I've heard no serious objections to this. I drew the attention of the revolutionaries to their own delusional state of mind, and Lavrov confined himself to the response that such accusations were allegedly "unfounded". But, ignoring the considerations given to me specifically, this accusation fails to touch what I've revealed. Did Lavrov only skim through Taine, who traced the state of the human mind at one of the most consequential historical moments?[80] Let him read, for example, the social novels of Roni[81], who studied the French revolutionary milieu... No, one can simply dismiss these observations with the flippant objection that "they are unfounded". All this shows is that the person protesting either does not know the facts or refuses to consider them.

Further, for example, I pointed out the ambiguity of the very concept of *revolution* among my opponents. Lavrov said a great deal in response, but I challenge anyone to understand whether he considers the revolutionary process a type of change, a violent coup, or a symptom even he doesn't fully grasp. How can we argue, how can we reason, if the basic concepts are shrouded in fog? What goes on in the heads of Lavrov's students, who consider it a duty to agree with him, but who are obviously not gifted enough to understand that which makes no sense? Leaving the heart of the dispute without clarification, my opponent has instead gone into endless matters of lesser importance, tagging my assertions in a purely mechanical fashion by repeating: "no, this isn't so", "no, you yourself are that way". Is this really a work of fresh, innovative, creative thought?

---

[80] **(*Ed.*)** Refers to Taine's three-volume work, *The French Revolution*.
[81] **(*Ed.*)** Refers to Joseph Henri Rosny (1856-1940), a French writer influential in the development of the science fiction genre.

I don't see any thought here, and I say this in all seriousness, not as an adversary but as a reader; I don't see where Lavrov makes a single real objection. Here, for example, is an extract on parliamentarism (which now constitutes the object of desire for Lavrov's students, if not for Lavrov himself). "L.A. Tikhomirov, relying on the fact that, relative to the objectives of the socialist system [?], parliamentarism is "extremely unsatisfactory" [he quotes my phrase. - *L.T.*], finds it possible to condemn it in comparison with autocratic government" (p.26). What a miserable objection!

In fact, I relied on nothing of the sort. I made no comparisons between socialism and parliamentarism, and in fact, I tend to think this would be something like comparing the rings of a triangle and a bell. I simply said that from the point of view of carrying out the everyday tasks of government, parliamentarism, while having some other advantages, is worthless as a *system of government*. I spoke about democratic parliamentarism and I would repeat it all again. It is puzzling to me how Mr. Lavrov, having lived for twenty years in parliamentary countries, does not see the innumerable shortcomings of this political system of universal impotence, introducing into politics a mercantile principle of free competition, making power the subject of speculation, and culminating with governmental anarchy. It only occurs to Lavrov to criticise parliamentarism in comparison with the "socialist system". Let him read Chapter 15 of the book *Du contrat social* by Rousseau (*Des deputes ou representants*[82]), and he will see that even the purest democrats, who had no clue about the "socialist system", consider the representative system to be worthless. The parliamentary practice of the 19th century, while adding nothing in favour of this system, demonstrated its flaws with greater clarity. Lavrov appears to have "overslept" and missed all the thought produced in this century.

He directs all his energy against me on the question of *autocracy* (pp.21-25). His argument is as follows. Lived phases are repeated neither in the sociological nor biological organism. "A sole power, subordinate to no law," is a lived phase. Normally, it could only survive in primitive eras. Since nations have undergone an internal levelling, the idea of an impersonal law has emerged, and autocracy

---

[82] **(Ed.)** Fr: *Deputies or representatives.* That is, chapter XV of the popular 1762 Enlightenment work, *The Social Contract*, by Jean-Jacques Rousseau (1712-1778), a Genevan philosopher.

has begun its "fated" collapse. Lavrov knows all too well that even after Numa Pompilius[83], the people resorted to autocracy to save themselves from the exploitative oligarchy of the Roman Republic, from the feudal lords of the Middle Ages and up to our times (p.23). "The idea of autocracy," he says, "is *as if* experiencing a rebirth". Not only that, he knows that such eras occur precisely so that reforms can come about which better allow the rule of law to function. Nevertheless, he claims that autocracy has fallen again and again. This is to assert that Lavrov's opinion is the rule, while all history is an exception! What does he mean by "fall"? The point, you see, is that the revival is only *apparent*, since life *gives new content to the old form*. Does Lavrov believe that life does not do the same thing with old republican forms? Recognising the great historical role of the autocracy, it is in this role that he sees its future collapse, since, by enacting reforms and implementing the rule of law, the autocracy makes of itself an internal contradiction and begins to fall apart... Finally, we arrive at the emergence of socialism, and here already (the revolutionary philosopher assures us) no further "revivals" are possible. "Here, the only possible political form is extreme democracy, which *would eliminate both the current parliamentarism and contemporary state and legal forms*" (p.24).

It is sad to see these pitiful phrases from the silver-haired "scientist". But let's take them in order. First, it is false that the archetype of the true autocrat should be sought almost in the conventions of the prehistoric era. Was Rurik[84] more autocratic than Peter the Great? Does precise *knowledge* inform Lavrov's historical viewpoint here? The inaccuracy of autocracy's definition, its equation with despotism, the opposition of autocracy and legality, all constitute further foundations of Lavrov's argument. But there isn't a single true utterance here. Who does not know that, in reality, *any* form of power is capable of *despotism*, be it monarchic, aristocratic or democratic! Likewise, *legality* is an equally necessary element in

---

[83] **(Ed.)** Numa Pompilius (753-673 BC): Second king of Rome. Given the context, Tikhomirov likely mistook him for Lucius Tarquinius Superbus, the seventh and final king of Rome whose tyranny resulted in the overthrow of the crown and the establishment of the Roman Republic in 509 BC.
[84] **(Ed.)** Rurik (830-879): Varangian chieftain considered to be the founder of the proto-Russian state, his family ruling over the Russian lands until the *Time of Troubles* in the 17th century, after which the Romanovs took power.

all forms of power. The difference between these forms is not at all in their respect for the law, nor their enforcement of the law, but only in the different *source* from whence the *law* comes. Under all forms of power, *everyone* is subject to the law, except for the source of power at the time of its functioning.

Thus, Lavrov's criticism rests entirely on confused concepts. In this I would include the inaccurate and muddled view of sole power, as if it were a *phase* in the development of the idea of power. In fact, power has several basic *forms* that all evolve, contend with and displace one another, and in general, the basic sociological forms (like their biological counterparts) do not perish, but only outlive their various lived phases. Sole power is not itself a "phase", but just one of these basic forms which, like all others, has its own "phases". True, some of its phases become obsolete, but new ones appear instead. For a long time, I could scarcely think of anything stranger than the "objection" to new content animating sole power. This is not an *objection*, but an argument *in favour* of the autocracy! After all, the vitality of an institution is precisely measured by its ability to adapt to conditions and function with renewed vigour amid changing circumstances. If, according to Lavrov himself, the whole history of mankind, from the beginning to the present day, represents continuous "revivals" of autocracy, which adapts to new conditions and is itself a progressive force in every instance, on what basis can we conclude that this form has become obsolete?

If the past allows us to conclude anything about the future, should we not instead conclude that peoples will now turn to autocracy to solve the new questions of life?

There remains only one card left to play; "incompatibility with the ideals of socialism". Lavrov is a very fortunate man if at least he understands what he means by the "ideals of socialism", but in any case, it's obvious that such ideals, as sketched by Lavrov, are incompatible not only with autocracy, but with all contemporary state and legal forms, something he admits. Consequently, from this point of view the autocracy "has been outlived" no more so than parliamentarism or the most "progressive" federal republic...

What did Lavrov prove with this point, where he concedes the broader argument? Was this his intention? No. He wants to overthrow the autocracy but has only justified its rejection to those who would abolish *the state itself*. For those who do not want to abolish the state?

For such people, Lavrov's argument speaks *only* in favour of autocracy. Was this what he wanted to achieve?

And now, people whose prophets operate under such logic and such incomprehension of history, imagine that they are in possession of a kind of "science", "intellect"!..

I would defend my moral right to think, even if I came into conflict with the leading thoughts of mankind. But in this case, such a misfortune did not befall me. I came into conflict with the stratum and worldview which have a great deal of self-righteousness and conceit, and nothing more. By departing from them, I did not move backwards but forwards, in terms of maturity of thought, truth, and the good of the country. For me, this has long been clear, but after the period of emigrant polemics it will become, perhaps, clearer for others, at least for those who are able to evaluate what they have seen and heard. I would like to think that an honest assessment of the opinions and facts in question will, after this, attract more attention from the revolutionaries themselves, who only need drive away the fog of sophism and the commonplace in order to understand how all their activities are unworthy of a sober, adult person.

Has the time not come for this?

Whatever the case, it came for me. It came precisely because I started to think, study, take advantage of the intellectual work done in progressive countries, and I remain convinced that most of those who reproach me would end up following in my footsteps, if only they wished to learn, think and observe.

BEGINNINGS + ENDS

'LIBERALS' + TERRORISTS

Part One

"When Christians forsake a Christian society
There follows rebellion or revolution"

Ivan Aksakov[85]

Speech at the Slavic Charity Society, 1881

The acute consequences of an erroneous worldview appear only when it has matured to its logical conclusions. Until this maturation occurs, it manifests itself in forms that are innocuous in appearance, fearful to nobody. It is precisely this aspect which proves most dangerous, when worldviews are in their period of maturation, their quiet, secret development. They inspire no terror and provoke no energetic opposition from opponents. People, in their indifference, remain aloof, and simply observe as points of view are instilled in them or their children from which they would turn away in fear if they understood what ends these principles engendered. Only a few discerning minds play in vain the tragic role of Cassandra.[86] Their warnings are dismissed as the delirium of madmen, only to be paid attention to for amusement. In such an environment, the evolution of the triumphant idea continues to broaden, with a wider range of action, finally developing forces that nothing can crush, until at last this evil, having become triumphant, devours itself and its host country with it.

---

[85] **(Ed.)** Ivan Aksakov (1823-1886): Russian conservative publicist and founder of the Slavic Charity Society, which gave aid to Slavs under Ottoman rule in the Balkans. After becoming a staunch critic of Alexander II, his society was shut down until he returned to favour with the enthronement of Alexander III.

[86] **(Ed.)** According to Greek mythology, the daughter of Priam, king of Troy. She predicted disaster for the city but was cursed never to be believed.

In this progressive development, the worst thing is that every year an increasing number of people become *accustomed* to notorious viewpoints and gradually to their conclusions. At first, it seems dreadful and ridiculous to say: "Poland is upheld by disorder". They start instead with more harmless sentiments: "Well, to have our order would be worse than disorder" or: "You cannot make an idol out of order", etc. Once the audience is accustomed to a softened formulation, it is sharpened a little, then a little more, and so on. This does not arise out of sophisticated calculation, out of reason inspired by an evil will, but out of a pure absence of reason. Very few exceptionally farsighted minds are able to discern in advance the final conclusions of this worldview. But no matter how notorious an idea is sown among an unreasonable crowd, it will most certainly, step by step, come to realise its conclusion. Reason, able to foresee, will fight in advance and expose the very idea itself as' falsehood. A senselessness which fails to foresee a conclusion, will not fight; it will instead assimilate itself to the idea, get used to it as a mathematical axiom, and then, as its conclusion approaches, will involuntarily submit to it, even with aversion, as something inevitable. What is at first said, is eventually done? Perhaps it would be preferable if the earth did not hold us to itself, but this is the law of nature.

Question: "Is this precisely a law of nature? Is not nonsense at the root of any idea which concludes in the absurd or the criminal?"; such a question can be quite easily posed to the average mind among the multitudes, up until the point at which they come to see this idea as an absolute truth. Yet once their heart is completely hardened, the matter is finished. They are too weak to resist completing the circle of logic. No matter what calamities or absurdities result, they will only become further inclined towards a more straightforward implementation, that is, they will seek remedy not in criticising the fundamental, but in its more rigorous application. The constitutional monarchy performs poorly; then we shall try a republic, demolish all barriers to franchise, introduce the popular vote for all laws, devolve governmental power down to the smallest locality, implement the *liberum veto*[87], experiment with the ideas of modern anarchists who have already uttered the last word of "self-government" in the form

---

[87] **(Ed.)** Lat: *Free veto.*

of *l'autonomie individuelle*[88]; in a word, we will try every conclusion which follows from our idea until the very last outworking, whereupon we can finally knock our forehead against the wall, able to exclaim: "What an idiot I was, when all along it was the idea itself which was nonsense; is it any wonder nothing has come of it!"

Unfortunately, this demonstrative tuition in real time comes at too high a price. It puts at stake the very existence of the nation.

It is therefore preferable for us not to allow for any great length of time in which the falsehood might mature. We would benefit if, the multitudes having not yet embraced and been blinded by this falsehood, something of its conclusion was exposed, while there are still enough good men in this country who could take advantage of our instruction.

---

[88] **(Ed.)** Fr: *The autonomous individual.*

Part Two

Russia came to know this direction during the 70s. With the exception of the Time of Troubles, we have faced no greater test. It was not a Mongol yoke, an enemy invasion, a disaster of external origin, but a manifestation of ourselves, our own spiritual corruption, where

You find the root of evil in yourself
And the heavens can be blamed for nothing.[89]

Is this disease... terminal? Is it to the greater glory of God? The issue is decided by us, our ability to grasp the direction and come to terms with its reality. If we don't have enough sense even for this, the heavens really can't be blamed for anything. With some strange mistake, a blunder inexcusable from the point of view of the revolutionary, and from the point of view of the government a bizarre, inexplicable indulgence; the "progressive" "cultural movement" was so emboldened that from its impregnable domain of legal activity, it went into the open field. Aposiopeses[90] of all kinds: on the one hand, we cannot admit, but on the other we cannot help but confess, Aesopian[91] language and wedge-shaped liberal logic upon which not only the simple-minded layman, but even the devil would break his leg; all of this is discarded, conclusions instead being drawn directly, boldly, in human language, word not diverging from deed. The whirlwind spins with all the force available for the handful of victims caught within it, and in a few years, it comes to draw a complete, logical circle. The ends met the beginnings.

---

[89] **(Ed.)** From the poem, *Yest' vremya...* (There is a time...) by Mikhail Lermontov (1814-1841), a Russian writer in the Romantic tradition.

[90] **(Ed.)** A figure of speech wherein a sentence is deliberately broken off and left unfinished, the ending to be supplied by the imagination.

[91] **(Ed.)** From Aesop's Fables, a collection of morality tales traced to Ancient Greece, that is, language with a hidden meaning behind an innocent exterior.

Loud, spiralling, it crushed what it could, its verse coming like a question: "Do you like? Is this what you wish? Or something even bigger? If so, gentlemen, by all means continue, for this is not my concern. Only procure more material for me".

We stand and ask ourselves: "Is this what Russia wants? And to whom can she appeal if she does not understand, if she will not change? In the end, a nation that wants to exist must have some common sense. If she cannot understand even the clearest facts playing out before her eyes, does justice not require her to clear her place in history for someone more capable?"

Part Three

Leaving the future for the future, one cannot help but conclude that, in the past as much as the present, the most harmful development was not and is not the existence nor preaching of unbridled revolutionaries, but rather that a great many people for themselves and others posit revolutionary sermons as something entirely divorced from the general outlook of the intelligentsia. This is carried out due to actual misunderstandings, a desire to mask propaganda on the part of some, and for others it comes down to the influence of an insulted patriotism, unable as they are to swallow thoughts of the true depth of the collapse of political meaning for a whole, huge stratum of society. For whatever reason, this is a mistake or a lie that is beneficial only to people who are secretly continuing to breed revolutionaries.

The truth, no matter how tragic, is more profitable when it is known and clearly rendered.

Of the generation of the 70s, anyone can scold anyone, I will not contradict him. But all these censures should fall hardest on the spiritual fathers, the educators, who created the generation of the 70s, who doomed it to sterility and death in advance. It was truly "a generation cursed by God," as one poet said of it. [92] Strictly speaking, it was prepared to such an extent that there was almost nothing for purely revolutionary propaganda to impress upon it. This is the reason they were taken in so easily. No mediocrity was capable of leading them, and any small, capable revolutionary triumphed unconditionally wherever he appeared.

---

[92] **(Ed.)** I was unable to find this reference.

Part Four

Between 1873 and 1874, a certain Dmitry Rogachev was sought throughout Russia. He gained celebrity status for investigators, and indeed; he brought many to the path of revolution. I remember that I was extremely surprised to hear about these exploits: I knew Rogachev very well. He was an easy-going type, a muscle man, a hero of habit, but so simple, so ignorant, that the Tchaikovsky Circle, with all its personal sympathies for Rogachev, did not dare to accept him among its membership. Who and where would be convinced of anything by him? Subsequently, having been arrested, he began to write his memoirs and sweated hard over them. Some of the lawyers who had the occasion to see this work of the "famous propagandist", who won the place among the five "greatest propagandists" during the trial of the 193[93], were disappointed to the point of pity. Indeed, it is hard to imagine anything more, I won't say literarily mediocre, but vacuous, without one solitary spark of content. This man, who travelled half of Russia, visited various circles of the intelligentsia, workers' artels[94], among the barge-haulers, non-conformists, etc., noticed nothing, remembered nothing, as if he had in truth been buried in the ground for these past two or three years.

And he "seduced" the youth by the dozens! It is clear that in reality he seduced nobody. He only took the *ready*. He was but a walking banner around which they gathered.

Someone writing in the old émigré magazine[95] (in this case a former naval officer, as it says in the article) recalled, not all too badly, the scene of his "seduction". The infamous Sukhanov[96]

---

[93] **(Ed.)** See pp.ii-iii.

[94] **(Ed.)** Early worker cooperatives which became popular in Russia after the emancipation of the serfs in 1861.

[95] *Bulletin of the People's Will.* T.M. S. 64.

[96] **(Ed.)** Nikolai Sukhanov (1851-1882): Russian revolutionary and member of the People's Will Executive Committee. He was arrested in 1881 and executed after the *Trial of the 20*, due to his rank as a naval fleet lieutenant.

(national criminal, later executed) was holding a political conference. He was a no less infamous orator than Zhelyabov.[97] He quite unashamedly outlined his own plans.

"In response to the first words: "We are revolutionary terrorists," reported one eyewitness, everybody seemed to flinch and look to each other in bewilderment. From then on, they listened with undivided attention. The carefree, somewhat cheerful gathering, as if by magic, became like a den of conspirators. When the speech was over, lively conversation began, various plots of the most terrorist nature being devised. If an outsider had entered then, he would have concluded that he had stumbled upon a gathering of zealous terrorists. "He" the witness exclaims, "would not have believed that *an hour before, all these people for the most part did not think about politics, and some had even censured terrorists themselves*".

How can we explain this scene? Did the speaker reshape his audience in half an hour? Such nonsense is shameful to even consider. The eyewitness himself clearly explains how he and his comrades "did not think about politics" or "had censured". The truth is very simple.

"Filled with *sincere hatred*, etc.," he says, "we did not believe in the possibility of an imminent coup in Russia; our desire for activity was reduced to the desire to work in the zemstvo. We dreamed of, having retired, getting into the zemstvo, and through it waging a struggle with the government. We did not believe in the power of the revolutionary party" (p.61).

So, what kind of "well-meaning" people did the propagandist seduce! They did not believe in power and therefore intended to become well-meaning supporters of dissident positions! There appears a dextrous man who stupefies for a minute, who puts on a good face; and our "well-meaning" begin to make plans of "the most terrorist nature". Hand on heart, how much did the propagandist do? Is it something inherent, or arising from those who educated this youth in such a way, that they immediately decided to join the revolutionary action as soon as they believed, even if mistakenly, in its possibility?..

And what action! *Behold its* forms and manifestations!

---

[97] **(*Ed.*)** Andrei Zhelyabov, see p.iv.

Part Five

My childhood apparently featured no predictors of a revolutionary temperament. In our family, we believed in God, and not in the simplified, Lutheran sense that I see so often nowadays, but in a truly Orthodox sense. For us, both the Church and the sacraments existed. I still remember the feeling with which I prayed during the Cherubikon[98], confident that at such a moment the Lord would least wish to refuse this prayer of a child. I truly loved Russia. For what reason I do not know, but I felt pride in her mass, considering her the preeminent country in all the world. Vaguely, but warmly, I felt the ideal of the almighty tsar, the ruler of everything and everyone… Just so did they pass me from childhood into the hands of social influences.

Is it really necessary to relate how quickly all of this collapsed?

The "spirit of the age", by whatever unintended mechanism, snuck into my early education, not so much in the sense of *what* was being taught, but the *way* in which it was taught. In school, there's nothing to tell, it reigned supreme at that time (1864-1870).

In a kind of reaction against the old "do not reason, obey" we were all led by the rule: "do not obey, reason".

Our educators decidedly failed to understand that the first quality of a truly developed mind is an understanding of the limits of its power, and that insofar as reasoning is necessary within these limits, it is indecent even for an intelligent person outside of them, where precisely the mind makes one simply "obey", sincerely, knowingly submit to authority.

In our time, we did not understand that reasoning recklessly, beyond the bounds of personal or even human powers, leads to confusion and, in fact, fails even to eliminate submission to

---

[98] **(Ed.)** The troparion normally sung at the Great Entrance during the Byzantine liturgy.

authorities; only that our submission becomes unconscious, and not to those who we might readily recognise as the highest, but to whatever can flatter us and exploit our weaknesses.

From infancy, they explained everything to us, used proofs, taught us to believe that only what is clear to us is true. It was not the cultivation of an independent mind, but a bull-headed one. I remember, for ten years I read *The World Before the Creation of Man*[99], and with what trepidation! How afraid I was that the author would destroy my shrine! But it never occurred to me that I could not begin to solve the question: who is right, Moses or Zimmerman? Getting older, I directly told myself: "Let me be mistaken, but I judged for *myself*, and it is not my fault if I could not reason better!" It never occurred to me that if I really arrived at all conclusions *myself*, then I would have remained a savage for a century. This proud "judged for himself" simply meant: he took from people, but only the weakest, simplest, easiest to digest. And if he had not judged "himself", but instead taken the recommendations of the great historical authorities, he would have taken the strongest, the most true, and yet this is hardest to swallow, for it is what you "yourself" will not reach unless you live a thousand years.

With this exaggerated trust in the liberties of our minds, we were, less than any other generation, able to truly use them, since their ability to function was undermined by a lack of discipline. The very concept of the disciplined mind completely faded away at the school of my time (1864–1870). Our worst teachers were perhaps the least harmful. At least their lessons were taught boringly, unconsciously, forcing us to make some effort. Good teachers, meanwhile, were shot through with some measure of *interest*. We learned from them not what was needed, necessity as an attribute being replaced by what was interesting, what captivated *us*. We were not masters, but slaves of the subject. We learned not to wilfully direct our attention, but only to surrender to impressions. It was a complete loss of the courageous independence of the mind, the ability and inclination to *combat a subject* replaced with such relaxation, such effeminacy, a tendency to give in to interest, to whatever most stimulated the imagination; and at the same time, for the sins of our parents, the deepest faith in our

---

[99] **(Ed.)** This refers to an obscure 1865 book by F. A. Zimmerman, which contains an early version of the generally accepted history of primitive earth.

own minds and the truths they supposedly told us! One such tempering (or rather, **searing**) of the mind is enough to condemn a generation to sterility.

At the same time, this education necessarily cut us off from the old historical culture, from the aid of God and the efforts of billions of people developing on earth since the creation of the world. This culture is full of authorities, often incomprehensible. You can be joined to it either in complete naïveté, or with a strong mental constitution, built up in strength, mature, able to both dominate and obey. Our childish naïveté had evaporated, but in its place came reasoning, headstrong and flabby. The old culture became inaccessible to us from this moment on.

We would search for something new, something lighter, something we could shoulder ourselves, but there was nothing to be sought. It surrounded us from all sides. After all, it had created us. It was enough to **go with the flow**.

Part Six

Everything that I heard as a young man systematically undermined my childhood beliefs. I saw around me the performance of religious rites, but such performances were either insincere or done with embarrassment. An educated person either did not believe, or believed in conflict with his own convictions. **What mere boys, youths were not required to hear or read about religion!**

The books did not speak of Orthodoxy. They related the superstitions of Catholicism, the inconsistencies of Protestantism, the fanaticism of the clerics, even with the postscript that all of this did not apply to Orthodoxy. The mocking tone of this clause was all too clear, especially since materialism was now being preached openly. But if there is no God, if Christ was simply a man, of course it is not difficult to judge what Orthodoxy is.

I began reading Pisarev[100] very early; and where? My uncle was a very intelligent and educated person, a great devotee of the *Moskovskie Vedomosti* and, by the standards of that time, a conservative. Why did such a person check out *Russkoe Slovo* and leave it on his bookcase? Why did he let me sit for hours with my nose in such books? Of course, he would not be able to answer this himself. Be that as it may, Pisarev soon became by favourite tutor. With his instruction, everything went full steam ahead. For about fifteen years I believed in all kinds of "arbitrary origins", in Pouchet[101], Joly[102], Musset, etc. as solidly as I believed in the

---

[100] **(Ed.)** Dmitry Pisarev (1840-1868): Russian publicist and literary critic, leading writer of the nihilist magazine, *Russkoe Slovo* (Russian Word), which is here contrasted with the conservative *Moskovskie Vedomosti* (Moscow News).

[101] **(Ed.)** Félix-Archimède Pouchet (1800-1872): French naturalist, the most prominent opponent of Pasteur's germ theory. Pouchet believed that life spontaneously generated itself from non-living material.

[102] **(Ed.)** Nicolas Joly (1812-1885): French professor of physiology. He took up the scientific cause of Pouchet's spontaneous generation, along with his student, Charles Musset.

sphericity of the earth, or indeed the ignorance of Pasteur, the emptiness of Pushkin and the "obscurantism" of the Slavophiles. [103]

I am not one of those for whom the value of religion consists in its benefit to the state and more generally in its social significance. But such a paramount factor as religion cannot but have enormous social significance. The eradication within us of the concept of God, of the eternal goals of life, of the episodic nature of our earthly existence itself, left a huge void in our souls which it was imperative to fill, all the more so since despite all mutilations, we were still Russian. This need for a consciousness of one's connection with some eternal life, for the development of some kind of immortal ideal of truth, certainly had to be satisfied. And so arrived our surrogate, a faith in humanity, in social progress and the future earthly paradise of materialism. It was *faith*, not some product of persuasion, faith, although its occupation was that of a relatively worthless, ignominious faith which villainised our mental state. We regarded social forms not as everyday things, but as religious realities; we applied to them those aspirations that were prompted by our spiritual nature, aspirations for *universality* and *freedom*. Transferring religion to the material sphere of politics, we did not want to recognise in it any laws of the material world, no organic fetters, and by extension, no national development, no inevitable constraint on social forms, and as a result we inevitably became dissidents and revolutionaries.

V. Soloviev[104] reproached Danilevskii[105], as if his nationalism and the doctrine of historical types were contrary to Christian sense. On the contrary, Danilevskii, like any profound Christian, could not fall into the trap which is inevitable for non-Christian or semi-Christian sociologists. He clearly felt what in our life comes from this world and what does not. For him, the absolute, eternal and free, did not evaporate in man at the thought of the necessity and

---

[103] **(Ed.)** The Slavophile movement, beginning in the early 1800s, was a native form of Russian Romantic conservatism, opposed to westernisation.

[104] **(Ed.)** Vladimir Soloviev (1853-1900): Russian philosopher and theologian. He held eclectic political views, being sympathetic to European thought, and often clashed as much with conservative as liberal thinkers.

[105] **(Ed.)** Nikolai Danilevskii (1822-1885): Russian geopolitical theorist and the conservative ideologist of pan-Slavism. His major 1869 work, *Russia and Europe*, put forward a cyclical view of history in which distinct *historical types* rise and fall, and strongly grounded his view in natural phenomena.

conditionality of his earthly existence in the material, biological and social world, where there is race, nationality, and their fateful organic development. And thus, Danilevskii could consider the necessary, constraining laws of sociology and each person's submission to their objectivity, undisturbed in his analysis by unnecessary intrusions from the domain of pure spirit.

One particularly astute anarchist perfectly described to me the difference between his views and those of the Christian. In the world, he said, a new *religion* is brewing. Our scientists imagine they work for reason. Similarly, ancient scholars did not know they were only clearing the way for a new religion. Christianity divides a person into two halves; spirit and body. Christianity demeans the body, forces you to fight the flesh. We rehabilitate the body. Spirit is what it is. The body is holy; there are no bad motives in it. Obey it, do not resist it, let all its aspirations manifest freely, and they will emerge in a fraternal harmony of the desires of all mankind.

Drive nature through the door and she will fly out of the window.[106] They forgot God and created an idol from their flesh!

This, in fact, is why I must emphasise repeatedly the anti-Christianity of our new worldview. It created a new religion within us. This was true to such an extent that one branch of the 70s movement actually created its own sect, the so-called God-men.[107] A prominent figure along with the once famous Malikov[108] was Tchaikovsky[109], the same one whom the Circle selected as leader in almost all factions of the revolutionary movement in the following years. True, *God-manhood* set its principle as *non-resistance to evil*, and thereby sharply deviated from violent revolutionaries. But this is a difference that matters only to the police and the prosecutor's office, and not to someone who considers the issue from the point of view of Christian culture and the Russian national type. The deification of

---

[106] **(Ed.)** This plays on a quote from Danilevskii's book; "shut nature out the door, and it will come in the window". *Russia and Europe: the Slavic World's Political and Cultural Relations with the Germanic-Roman West* (2013). Bloomington, IN: Slavica, p.156.

[107] **(Ed.)** A minor pacifist cult, the *Bogocheloveki* (God-men) believed all men were literally God.

[108] **(Ed.)** Alexander Malikov (1839-1904): Russian nihilist, arrested for revolutionary activity in 1866. He subsequently joined the *Bogocheloveki*.

[109] **(Ed.)** Nikolai Tchaikovsky, see p.ii.

man, the transfer of religion to the social sphere was, in one form or another, completely inevitable after the Christian conception of the world was erased from us. And once we had transferred the absolute religious principle to the social field, we necessarily reacted negatively to everything conditional, that is, everything historical, national, everything that makes up the real social world.

In advance, we condemned this real world to death, in one form or another, by various means, condemned it from the moment we lost our personal God the Provider, still ignorant of the consequences of this loss.

Part Seven

The phenomenon that I speak of belongs not only to Russia, and perhaps even did not originate within her. But despite all the denationalisation of our educated stratum, it nevertheless retained something of its Russian properties, and, we should say, the characteristically Russian religious thirst. At the same time, ours differs from all the educated classes in Europe, without a doubt, by the worst outworking of its mind. It thus granted the widest possible manifestation of *social religiosity*. The late Count D. A. Tolstoy[110], with great accuracy, compared our revolutionaries, "resistors" or "non-resistors," with the convulsive sectarians of the medieval period. Reflecting on his own revolution, Louis Blanc[111] also sensed some kind of similarity, was looking for some root in the sectarianism of the Middle Ages, although the question remained obscure for him. In fact, there is no need for any *genetic* connection, and the history of our educated class perfectly proves this.

The transfer of religious concepts to the field of material social relations leads to an eternal revolution, endless because any society, no matter how it is remade, will be as unrepresentative of the absolute Eden as any modern or past societies. It is for this reason that the most advanced revolutionaries of the West took up the name of anarchists, and it is worth noting that Russian society, so meagre in intellectual power in other respects, gave Europe its two greatest theorists of anarchism: Bakunin[112] and Kropotkin.[113] Our idealists of the 40s are more or less anarchists, for the most part themselves not realising it.

---

[110] *(Ed.)* Dmitry Tolstoy (1823-1889): Russian statesman who occupied various government posts under Tsar Alexander II. A political conservative.

[111] *(Ed.)* Louis Blanc (1811-1882): French socialist politician.

[112] *(Ed.)* Mikhail Bakunin (1814-1876): Russian political philosopher and a chief ideologist of anarchism. He spent most of his life either in exile, prison, or directly participating in popular uprisings in Europe.

[113] *(Ed.)* Peter Kropotkin (1842-1921): Russian political philosopher. Like Bakunin, his anarchism meant that he spent most of his adult life in exile.

If Saltykov[114] (Shchedrin) knew how to draw conclusions from his infinitely negative worldview, he could give a hand not to Lavrov, not to the Social Democrats (they are all too little revolutionary for him), but only to the anarchist Kropotkin. Anyone who has ever observed European countries knows very well that our current, liberal notions of freedom, by their exaggeration, are precisely those adhered to by European anarchists, not liberals.

The cosmopolitanism of our educated class was destined to degenerate into something even worse. **The French or German anarchist hates modern society *in general*, and not specifically his own. In essence, our cosmopolitan is not even cosmopolitan; for in his heart, all countries are not the same, but all are more pleasant than his native land**. For him, the spiritual homeland is France or England, generally "Europe"; in relation to them he is not a cosmopolitan, but instead the most partisan patriot. In Russia, everything is so contrary to his ideals that the thought of Europe rouses a yearning in him. Our "progressive", educated person is able to love only the "Russia of the future", where there is no trace of the Russian.

We find that often there is an especially and truly hostile feeling towards Great Russia[115] in particular. This is natural, since in the end, only the genius of Great Russia created what we know as Russia. Were it not for Great Russia, especially Moscow, all of our outlying Russian regions would present the same picture of anonymised fragmentation as the rest of the Slavic world. Of all the Slavic tribes, it is only one, the Great Russian race, which possesses those instincts for great statecraft. Therefore, she arouses a special hatred in those who find disgusting everything in society that is historical and organic, all which is not arbitrary or accidental but necessary. Hence why historians like Kostomarov[116] were popular among us, he who

---

[114] **(Ed.)** Mikhail Saltykov-Shchedrin (1826-1889): Russian satirist writer. His attacks on the bureaucracy often led to his work being censored, but he never truly aligned with the far-left camp.

[115] **(Ed.)** An expression meant to refer to what Europeans simply call Russians, but to distinguish them from *White Russians* (Belarusians) and *Little Russians* (Ukrainians).

[116] **(Ed.)** Nikolai Kostomarov (1817-1885): Russian historian and popular writer in the Narodnik subculture. He often portrayed Little Russians as being a distinct nationality, more attuned to poetry and ideas of liberty than Great Russians.

made such efforts to dethrone the entire patriotic sanctity of Great Russia, destroying its Susanins[117], understanding nothing before the Time of Troubles so that in the end, he declared the era more likely to belong to Polish history than Russian.

By the time my generation was surrendered to society, a whole liberal culture had already been created, the negative, predominantly anti-Russian aspirations of which reached their zenith in the 60s. It was at this time that the young, brilliant lieutenant colonel of the General Staff (Sokolov[118], subsequently an emigrant) proudly declared before a court: "I am a nihilist and a renegade". Military youth joined Polish gangs to kill their compatriots for the cause of the restoration of Poland, as if choosing the motto: "where there is rebellion; there is the fatherland". The Russian liberal press approved this disgrace, and M.N. Katkov, with all the passion of the Russian feeling, in opposing such traitorous intoxication, has since remained forever himself a traitor and enemy to the liberal mind.

The Russia of my childhood dreams was vividly debunked. It turned out to be, "in the light of science", only a poor, ignorant, backward country, the whole merit of which was reduced to the desire to become like "Europe". There were other evaluations, but where to find them? In the most widespread literature, in the academy itself, liberal points of view reigned. We would have needed a particular blessing and an absolutely exceptional circumstance in order not to fall under their influence, which, from all sides, drove us to the cause of revolution.

---

[117] **(Ed.)** Ivan Susanin was a Russian national hero during the Time of Troubles. A peasant, he misled a group of Polish troops seeking to assassinate the first Romanov Tsar, taking them deep into the forest where they were never heard from again. Kostomarov considered him to be a fictional character.

[118] **(Ed.)** Nikolai Sokolov (1832-1889): Russian revolutionary writer employed by *Russkoe Slovo*. He was exiled in 1867 and subsequently fled abroad.

Part Eight

Many cannot understand this. What commonality is there between the humble liberal and revolutionary extremes? Such is the view of those who think only of the liberal *programme*. Of course, revolutionary extremes do not stem from the positive demands of the liberals; the revolutionaries themselves mock them as stupid insincerities. Revolutionary extremes stem from the *general outlook*, which produces on the one hand half-finished, half-hearted and sometimes Jesuitical liberal demands, and on the other, revolutionary aspirations which are quite logical and consistent. Our "progressives" create revolutionaries not with their insignificant liberal programmes, but with the propagation of their vulgar worldview. If they were to abandon this general outlook, they would simultaneously undermine their liberal aspirations, which themselves would appear ridiculous, and revolutionary aspirations, which would come to resemble not *extremism*, but *insanity*. As long as the "progressives" retain their worldview, they will inevitably create revolutionaries. Willingly or not, they will cultivate a spirit among the youth most suitable for revolution, and even suggest to them courses of action, based upon their false characterisation of all that surrounds them.

Part Nine

There is no need here to elaborate on the literary influences of the 60s. They are known to everyone first-hand, and the modern public even tends to exaggerate their harmfulness, that is, in saying that the liberals and radicals etc. of that decade were more harmful than today's. I don't see it; but at present, alongside liberal dissidents, there are many nationalists whose voices are equally audible. At that time however, the only thing which could be heard was the din of the liberal choir, drowning out any other voices. Thus, their influence was stronger.

Our theoretical ideas, imparted to us by what was then called "science" not only in countless popular articles on the natural sciences, history, etc., but also by our educational institutions themselves, consisted of a negative attitude towards the societal structure of Russia, especially its model of government etc. Evaluations in literature and popular culture of the present reality in Russia settled the matter. As a boy and a young man, I lived through the era of reforms which are *today* extolled by liberals. However, at that time, I absolutely heard not a single good word about these same reforms. Then, nothing was being done as it should have been. Whatever the government touched, it spoiled. Instead of depicting the gracious sovereign, who cares so much for the needs of society, surrounded by love, care, the radiance of wisdom, in those days the liberals only complained and gave the impression that the government was "making concessions", but ones which were "insufficient". Liberals who are in fact only "liberal", who do not have a support for anarchy at heart, would never have permitted themselves such asinine behaviour, completely inconsistent with their party interests. Instead of supporting a government that was amenable to them, instead of informing us that only such a liberal government can rule well, the grumbling of the liberal only prepared the enemies of the government, and we, the youth, involuntarily absorbed the idea that a government of any kind, even the most liberal, would still be ineffectual. From my early youth, I heard only that Russia was ruined, on the eve of bankruptcy, that there was nothing in it but despotism, confusion and plunder; this was said with such unanimity, with such an absence of dissenting voices, that only after traveling abroad and being able to compare our monarchical order with the republican, could I finally understand the absurdity of such declarations. But back then, without knowing anything, with the inexperience of youth, it was the truth, it was impossible not to believe it.

But surely not everyone in Russia was a liberal? Of course not. There were, thank God, a lot of people of the "old culture", and I'm not just speaking of self-serving "serf-holders". I remember people who were very educated, humane. Such would not be an inaccurate description of my late father. But then, his was a strange era. There were improvements in conditions. However, it was precisely the hearts of people *then* which could provide the greatest moral pillar to our government, independent of any improvement. My father was quite the monarchist and in me laid the embryos of monarchist sympathies, but with what? With stories of the "era of Nicholas".[119] So great an impression was left on me by these warm tales of an austere, majestic time which could hold its banner high, that I never ceased to love the *personality* of Emperor Nicholas, even at the height of my rejection of the *system*. Why did my father not find the same warm feeling as a guarantor of our "improved" age? He did not have serfs, nor would he have wanted to have them. Generally, he approved of the reforms, not condemning directly even a single aspect. But, apparently, the new era did not complement his Russian Orthodox feeling. It left him cold. The same was true for others. They were not theorists, but simply felt that the new age, with all its improvements, was striving somewhere in the wrong direction. Thanks to the particulars of the era, Russia thus did not receive protection and support from those who would normally have done so without interest, without conditions, who would have been devoted to her government and moral purity, and who would have the greatest capability of influencing the youth... I repeat, it was an unhappy, doomed generation, cut off, seemingly in a deliberate and systematic

---

[119] (*Ed.*) That is, the reign of Nicholas I, which lasted from 1825 to 1855.

way by some mysterious force, from everything that could save it from perdition.

Part Ten

With an exceptionally simplified worldview, and with little work to do, our development did not take long. At the age of about eighteen or nineteen, the process was completed. Possessed of great self-confidence, and oftentimes a considerable store of acquired knowledge, we in fact remained very much uncultivated and ignorant. We did not know a single fact in its true completeness and versatility. The various points of view with which the teachers of mankind have tried to illuminate life in this way and that, were known to us only by name, in a distorted form. The world, without perspective, without shades, fell apart before us into two clearly defined domains. On the one hand; superstition, darkness, despotism, disasters, and on the other; science, reason, light, freedom and earthly paradise. In this mental state, the majority of us were frozen, probably never to thaw out.

But the real world does not in fact contain anything absolute, neither light nor darkness; it is all woven from shades, degrees. The absolute is the property of a completely different world. Transferring this religious concept to the world of conditionality, we found ourselves in complete contradiction with reality.

While we were still on the cusp of adulthood, this contrast did not weigh so depressingly upon us. Our minds were otherwise occupied, which dampened the effects. We could still be like "youth", in high spirits. When this ended, a period of severe anguish and inner emptiness began.

That which we recognised as truth and reason was nowhere to be found in reality; what was seemed like so much evil and nonsense. This was a heavy blow in itself. It led to a choice: either to live absent any moral content, conscious that our lives served nothing righteous and true, or to declare war on everything in existence. The decision was not easy. Yet, our situation at that time was worse. When we decided to "declare war", it turned out that we did not understand well what and who exactly we were declaring it against.

Indeed, what and whom exactly to destroy? What in particular were we to fight, what realities and what personalities? It would have been easy to discern if the world really was how we imagined it. If, on the one hand, there was a villainous exploiter, heartless, immoral, and on the other hand, the virtuous proletarian whom he devoured, it would not be difficult to understand upon whom to throw ourselves. But my first youthful encounters with life showed me something different. The very first businessman I met, who had such lovely young daughters with whom we danced merrily to the piano, did not fit my definition of a villain. He was even a very humane person, I heard that he gave a lot. The first proletarian whom I recognised was very difficult to define as a "victim of society". He was an ancient drunkard who extorted handouts through threats of scandal. Society itself was his victim. I saw the peasants and did not recognise them as my suffering and oppressed "people". I saw an official, a priest, a monk, and did not grasp the theoretical "evil" in them. Subsequently, in the course of conducting propaganda, we constantly found workers already "spoiled", found in them "bourgeois inclinations", "possessiveness", "a desire for luxury", and to find the real suffering people we always had to look further, to another place.

In life, essentially, there was a great deal of evil, suffering and oppression that we, with our simplified world outlook, could have imagined. Only, there was *neither evil nor good* visible to us. Our concepts were so alien to reality that it was impossible to use them as a guide to good or evil. We needed to fight, but with what exactly there was no way of knowing. What to wish for in the distant future (something which was of course also fantastical), we knew very well. But what to desire, what to strive for now, in the present, remained obscure.

Not only did theory come into conflict with reality, but it simply did not touch it, for good or ill, slipping through it like a ghost. A generation with a better mindset would immediately have suspected their ideas of complete absurdity and undertaken a radical revision of their entire intellectual position. We could not bring to bear questions or thoughts on such a tension. We instead simply felt that we were faced with some kind of smokescreen. What to wish for? What to prepare for? It was precisely the "twilight of the soul" when the "object of desire is gloomy" ...

To this situation I am accustomed,

But neither angelic nor demonic language
Could clearly express it:[120]

There were many cases of suicide at our university. Today they like to explain them with "overwork", borrowing from the Latin language. I know not whether this is the case today, but then it was a product of emotional emptiness, an ignorance of life's purpose. I know this all to well, since I myself was afraid in the acute moments of the "twilight of the soul". This intolerable state led to complete nervous breakdown, to a readiness to throw oneself into any kind of whirlpool, as long as it presented even the slightest chance to find a clear object of desire.

One cannot imagine a state of mind more favourable for the reception of revolutionary programmes.

---

[120] **(Ed.)** Again, from the poem, *Yest' vremya...* (There is a time...) by Mikhail Lermontov.

Part Eleven

At that time, revolutionaries in the strict sense of the word, that is, revolutionaries with a programme, conspirators, were almost non-existent. I speak here of a turning point reached between the 60s and the 70s.

Since 1866, conspirators had nearly melted away. At the forefront was the consciousness of the impossibility of revolution in the near future. The revolutionary spirit was transformed almost entirely into a kind of "cultural effort". Conspiracies, rebellion; all of this was premature. There was a need to spread *knowledge*. And this knowledge spread abundantly. In this particular era (the end of the 60s and the beginning of the 70s), there were many translations of all kinds of stories, revolutionary accounts, works of various kinds of socialists, etc. Lavrov, then a Russian subject, although administratively expelled, wrote his famous *Historical Letters,* a tract which long remained the gospel of the revolutionaries. A number of books appeared, such as *The Proletariat in France*, a translation of Marx, the writings of Lassalle[121], the books of Vermorel[122] such as *The Men of 1848* or *The Life of Marat*, the latter, a complete apology for Marat, was forbidden but widely read; Louis Blanc published in Russian the first volume of his *Revolution*[123]; Flerovsky's *The Condition of the Working Class in Russia* was a huge success.[124]

---

[121] **(Ed.)** Ferdinand Lassalle (1825-1864): Prussian jurist and socialist philosopher.

[122] **(Ed.)** Auguste-Jean-Marie Vermorel (1841-1871): French publicist who was mortally wounded during the siege of the revolutionary *Paris Commune*. The book mentioned was an apology for Jean-Paul Marat (1743-1793), the most famous journalist of the French Revolution, whose writings led to the execution of many during that time.

[123] **(Ed.)** This refers to Blanc's 1847 book, *Histoire de la Revolution Française* (History of the French Revolution).

[124] **(Ed.)** This book by the Russian sociologist, Vasily Bervi-Flerovsky (1829-1918), was a strong influence on the development of early Marxism.

There were a lot of such books, and all could be obtained. We were told: you need knowledge, and for this, you need to read. We read, and all the books said the same thing with complete unanimity. It turned out to be a total illusion (one which was, without a doubt, sincerely shared by the figures of the "cultural effort" themselves), as if the revolution was being precisely led by "science".

The successes of this movement were enormous. Subsequently, Zhelyabov was quite right when he said with sadness: "we live in our capital". Indeed, already in 1880, a shrewd person could not help but see that the terrorist era was only surviving, to put it bluntly, by "burning through" its capital, something which had already started to dwindle. Yet, in the 60s, capital was only accumulating in a widespread and successful fashion.

The work which produced this fruit, however, only strengthened our fundamental, negative worldview. It still provided no guide to *life*. Then appeared, in the form of a pale shadow of our sought-after solution, the *association* movement, a desire to found schools, libraries, etc. But we say precisely a shadow of the solution because, in essence, what is revolutionary about associations, schools, libraries? All these things, under certain conditions, can even be powerful levers for strengthening the most conservative principles. However, we could only have thrown ourselves into this activity, broadly and deeply, had our fundamental ideas not been so unconditionally negative. The thought was already percolating within us then, having arisen independently from logic: that "any piecemeal improvements will only strengthen the existing system". Why on earth would we devote our efforts to them?

But then, is not all revolutionary work an exercise not in strengthening, but destruction? Such was not perceived. The thought of a direct revolution, rebellion, conspiracy seemed chimerical. Nechayev[125], a quite exceptional fanatic, could only put together his secret society with lies and the most terrible despotism, the exposure and detonation of which came from the youth itself, a most fearsome reaction against conspiracy. In 1870, it was impossible to even hint at "organisations" with revolutionary goals. Without further discussion, such talk would be considered the direct work of an agent

---

[125] (*Ed.*) Sergey Nechayev, see p.ii.

provocateur. Nechayev himself was considered to be a police agent until he was extradited and convicted.

The conspirators, one might say, did not exist. The influence of the emigration was also negligible. Herzen[126] had long since pulled back, as if with some squeamishness, from "nihilism". Young people were orbiting around Bakunin, but there were no tangible reverberations in Russia. Lavrov did not yet exist, and when he appeared, even after fleeing abroad, he was still engaged only in the incitement of students in Zurich. Kropotkin (who has never, it should be noted, had any significant influence among Russians) was then still engaged in geological studies in Finland. Something like *Russian Affairs* was published abroad, I remember hearing, but to this day I've never seen it.

The influence of the emigration was negligible, virtually zero.

Considered in its totality, the transition period lasting from the 60s to the 70s was, more than any other I have witnessed, a lull in directly revolutionary thinking. For the first two years, I don't even remember a single conversation about politics at the university, and in student apartments such talk was dull, infrequent and boring, with many being made uncomfortable by the proposal: "Let's do more than drink, gentlemen". Back then they drank very hard. Most students thought exclusively of a "career". Others yearned for but never found their place in the world. In any event, the silence was absolute.

In hindsight, there was nothing worthwhile in *this* silence. You can place no reliance on young people when they are lifeless, but when they are enlivened by a healthy rejuvenation, they wake up, they are cheerful, they build all kinds of great plans for themselves, but these are not plans which overturn the existing order but develop its foundations. Categorically, I will never affirm the well-intentioned nature of those Russian youth who think only of their career, etc., especially if at the same time there is a general, progressive decay to be noted. This is a sure sign that their ideals are sick, and therefore do not find clear application in life, something which leads young people to try not to think about them. But this lack of thinking does not remedy the primary issue; *spiritual emptiness...*

---

[126] **(*Ed.*)** Alexander Herzen (1812-1870): Russian-Jewish writer influential upon the *Narodniks*. A partisan of agrarian socialism, he wrote most of his works abroad, only to become politically disillusioned in Europe.

One fine day, all these "careerists," you see, almost without exception, arrange some ridiculous circumstance in which, for a damn eggshell, they stupidly, aimlessly burn their entire "career" to ashes. Meanwhile, those who have not delved into the psychology of mass movements will just shrug their shoulders, exclaiming: "Where did it come from? Could it have been foreseen?"

It comes from the "emptiness".

A young man will never live with a "career" in place of an ideal. He himself is mistaken when he takes such a position, which he flaunts as a dry scepticism. He has this pretence, but it is only an amusement. Once he inevitably tires of amusing himself, the longer he remains unsatisfied the greater his need for a moral content of life will be. It will expand until it reaches the proportion of a passion, blinding him to everything else. And then, beware!

Beware of its nature. The moral content of life provides only the active implementation of an ideal. What ideals lurk in the soul of a "careerist"? In the depth of his heart, does he have the ideal of the soul's salvation, of eternal life, of denying the flesh? Obviously not, otherwise he would not flaunt "careerism". Does he have the ideal of the fatherland's glory, of its dazzling development, of its mighty origins in the world? Obviously not, otherwise his personal aspirations would never have taken the form of careerism. No, in his soul will only be found a *denial* of life as it exists, such a contempt for it, such a conviction that it is worthless, as to arouse no desire to render service to it. Here is what you will find: a negative ideal, and therefore, a moral content of life sought in its application which can only be destruction. And the less developed the ideal is, the more *effortless* will be its search for moral content.

The most effortless path is precisely the most ludicrous. It does not consist in searching for something yourself (this would require some measure of spiritual work, effort), but in simply opening the soul up to a kind of zeitgeist, a flow, a nervous current, and allowing it to freely merge with such emptiness. This will not satisfy a properly cultivated person, because he has *his own* content, indignant against the influx of others'. However, the uncultivated has no such indignation, and his spirit is here filled with emptiness. He becomes a slave to this zeitgeist, and follows it everywhere, to all extremes, to all manner of absurdities, to all sorts of crimes, as if under hypnosis, as if both gutless and reckless.

Part Twelve

At this time of calm, the Tchaikovsky Circle was born in St. Petersburg. It seems this happened in 1871. I'm writing from memory, without aid, so an error in dates would be easy to make here. In any case, this circle, at first insignificant, and two years later possessing already enormous means of influence, did not, in theory, bring anything new. Tchaikovsky did what all the other "cultural figures" of the revolution did: he disseminated "knowledge", etc. There was nothing directly rebellious about this. But his circle turned a mass of youth from a simple passive object of "cultural work" into its active factor. This was its only distinction. The Tchaikovskys themselves grew out of the "Self-education Circle," and they systematically spawned such circles everywhere, first in St. Petersburg, then throughout Russia. Tchaikovsky took an active part in the publication and distribution of literature created by our progressive people of that time. His circle soon began to distribute so many books that any publishing company would envy it. He had few publications of his own; he bought most of his books on commission, distributing them among young people at a cheapened price, at a loss to himself, and compensating for those losses with fees and donations. The circles created by him took an active part in all this work. Young people not only "self-educated", but "educated" others, not only read, but also spread, were "enlivened" by some and "enlivened" others. The movement democratised, became the property not of the progressive aristocracy, but the progressive masses.

This is the true revolutionary significance of Tchaikovsky's Circle. He set up a number of leaders who would subsequently oversee the direction of the movement, but he did not create them, only letting them emerge. He was not the one to develop their ideas. However, he *stirred the masses*, brought them out from apathy, from inaction. But this was to do everything. When a mass with a revolutionary worldview is in a state of calm, it is enough to stir it up with anything, so long as it is stirred well. To do this, not every extreme method is always appropriate. Nechayev only knocked down youth, increasing their apathy. Tchaikovsky, by contrast, instinctively guessed how to measure his blows. He only slightly advanced the front of the general "cultural-revolutionary" movement, setting out only its immediate conclusions; they turned it into a mass movement, enlivened the masses. Once something like this is achieved, once the head has won out, the fundamentals of the worldview thus inevitably reach their logical conclusion, although the masses at first do not foresee it, even the "enliveners" themselves do not foresee it. Many of the Tchaikovsky loyalists turned away from what followed, but the events played out regardless.

At first, what came was not foreseen at all. We did not even call ourselves *revolutionaries*, but simply *radicals*. This name (a memory of our true origin) remained in the revolutionary milieu even at a time when terror was already raging in all its power. The name insulted the ears of emigrants very much, because abroad, between revolutionaries, the word *radical* was almost a swear word, such as how we say "liberal". Radicals, however, was still the self-descriptor used even by the People's Will. In the early days of the Tchaikovsky Circle, the educated tier found that, generally, our explicit consciousness, not being subject to any contestation that we weren't part of the most ordinary progressive front, found no clear need to invent or adopt any kind of special, distinctive moniker. Of course, we understood that we were revolutionaries in terms of our aspirations, but no more than all of those whose books we distributed. In terms of activity as well, we were nothing special, no different from the others. The revolution seemed to be something so magnificent that to apply this word to our petty work served only to vulgarise it.

Part Thirteen

The period of mass "self-education" and "book distribution" did not last long. Each of us soon became convinced that no matter how many books we read, they all said the same thing, this being exactly what we were already thinking. Thus, the excessive *self-education* of each individual soon ceased. All that remained in our hands after the dissolution of this personal duty was a public duty: the education of others, the distribution among others of books we no longer read. Pure *propaganda* was what remained in our hands, to which we had already become accustomed during the phase of self-education. The stratum of people thus engaged in propaganda grew stronger the more people moved beyond self-education. Being a specialist enterprise, propaganda naturally led us to consider building more advanced organs. With the participation of the Tchaikovsky Circle abroad, Lavrov's *Forward!*[127] appeared. The value of Lavrov himself should not be exaggerated. We forced him to rewrite the programme of the future organ three times.

The husk of self-education from which propaganda grew fell away. There was now only propaganda. But then propaganda experienced the same process. The propagandist, emerging from self-education, was met with the greatest success. After each encounter with a youth, he could say: *veni, vidi, vici.*[128] In fact, there was essentially no one to argue with, no one to win over, his whole arsenal of books having already advanced ahead of him. Everyone already had the same thoughts. Propaganda among the youth soon had little to accomplish; in the historical sense, it wasn't even so much propaganda as a general review of the existing revolutionary worldview.

It took about two years to produce what came next. At the end of this period, we were of completely the same mind as before.

---

[127] (*Ed.*) Lavrov's socialist journal, founded in 1872.
[128] (*Ed.*) Lat: *He came, he saw, he conquered.*

However, we realised now that we were everywhere; we were not fragmented but united, possessing in every city leaders we believed in. We thus tested our strength, became familiar with doing "political" things. We stirred and could no longer remain still.

The question of destroying the existing system and replacing it with a new one was specifically something that remained obscured by the same fog as two to three years before. But in the face of this question we could not, nor did we wish to, sit in passive longing. We rushed for an active way to uncover it.

Part Fourteen

Since that time, the revolutionary stratum began to acquire its own contours, gradually solidifying into the "party", creating its own social literature, programmes, subdivisions, and at times taking on a rather strong influence from the emigration. In general, it detached from the rest of the "intellectual" stratum. The liberals sometimes even entered into polemics with the revolutionaries, while the revolutionaries responded by abusively berating them. Despite all this, if revolutionaries became complete renegades from historical Russia during this time, I cannot in any way recognise them as renegades from the Europeanised segment of educated society. I positively affirm that there is not a single revolutionary trend (with the exception of *terrorism*) not rooted or reflected in legal literature, for the most part with the requisite censorship, sometimes not. The ideas of anarchism did not form a tight system, but spilled everywhere, without Bakunin's help. Our Russian ideas about personal freedom and public liberties from the very beginning were purely anarchist. I believe that not a single literature in the world has more anarchists than ours. Lavrov's doctrines were at first presented through the legal Russian press; subsequently, they were developed by so many publicists that I'm not even sure who I need to give chronological credit, though in the end it must be Lavrov. There is nothing to say about later events, these ideas even being transferred to poetry by the "famous" Nadson.[129] The Jacobinism of Tkachev[130] was also not news. The ideas of social democracy appeared in legal literature long before illegal literature. European democracy, Russian populism; all of it found exactly the same place in the propaganda of the "peaceful" and "rebellious".

---

[129] **(Ed.)** Semyon Nadson (1862-1887): Russian-Jewish poet. He produced very little, dying at a young age, but his poetry was popular among the far-left.

[130] **(Ed.)** Peter Tkachev (1844-1886): Russian revolutionary ideologist, close to Nechayev in his beliefs. After his exile in 1873, he furiously condemned peaceful activism on the part of the left in Russia.

Terrorism is an isolated trend. It is not a doctrine, but a *tactic*. And if we ask ourselves how such tactics could appear, what moral concepts were required, what assessments of the realities of Russia, then we will attach no importance to its apparent isolation.

However, the presence of all the foundations of revolutionary doctrine in the public consciousness, and, therefore, in the legal literature, is completely natural and inevitable, because they follow on from the general outlook of the Europeanised part of the educated stratum. A thought cannot but work itself out, even if it turns away from its final conclusion, or has it censored, something close is nevertheless achieved. A man who is bold or simply more consistent then only needs to add a few words; and so he is transformed from a "peaceful" leader into a revolutionary, from a "member of society" into an "enemy of society".

And purely liberal propaganda would have tried in vain to keep such a person "within boundaries". After all, it provides the premises, it proves their justice, and when it stops short before the conclusion, its students will either abandon liberalism with bewilderment or contempt. The liberal does not always deserve this contempt. Very often he stops before reaching the conclusion not because of cowardice or inconsistency, but because *common sense* cries out to him. But common sense (which is either instinct, or the result of fleeting, personal experience) cannot be passed on to another, especially the youth. Ideas, however, are transmitted.

The fault of such a man, possessing, for lack of a better term, common sense, is that he hesitates to apply this sense to his most theoretical concepts. Only then, having considered his ideas in a new light, could he successfully argue with the revolutionaries, not about the *conclusions* which they have quite rightly reached, but their mistaken *foundations*.

Part Fifteen

Revolutionary thought, the revolutionary mood, ripened to a state of maximum tension until it finally broke across the *movement*, which was captured by spasmodic convulsions for a whole fifteen years. This motion represents two large phases: at first it rushes "to the people" with the goal of... telling the truth, with a thousand intentions, all in the end reducible to the instigation of a popular revolution; in the second phase, revolutionaries, abandoning the people, endeavour to overthrow the government using the power of the intelligentsia; when these outbursts result in failure, the movement, exhausted, devoid of passion and confidence, degenerates on the one hand into an ugly constitutionalism, and on the other into a featureless, boring and probably fruitless belief in social democracy.

We should recall that in each of these distinct phases there were several different plans of action; different factions of propagandists and anarchist rebels, different attempts at self-appointment, attempts at action through our loyalists, attempts to initiate agitation for a constitution, attempts at conspiracies, attempts to "force concessions", attempts at "agrarian terror", etc.; and in assessing all this, one cannot but agree that for fifteen years this was a terrible mob which feverishly lurched from side to side, even to and from goals which were in opposition to each other, and this, as I have already said, was a *search*; a search that sought to connect one's revolutionary worldview with life as it was, a search which was obviously wholly unsuccessful, a constant butting up against impossibilities and absurdities, banging one's head against a wall, rushing to another rock to do the same, rushing again and again to wherever obstacles were not yet visible.

These people tried everything within the framework of their materialistic worldview, with its adoration of humanity and social forms, with the autocracy of the people, socialism, and the negation of historical necessity that follows from it.[131]

---

[131] Of course, I know that socialism, the so-called scientific socialism on which social democracy is built, recognises with no hesitation historical necessity and is completely devoid of religious character. But here, social democracy has always been negligible. In my opinion, even in Europe, with its first successes, it is shrinking before anarchism. Social democracy is the same compromise as bourgeois liberalism. Therefore, scientific socialism in our country is most widespread in the layers of the politically purely liberal, and our social democrats are the only revolutionaries who are sincerely ready to help the constitutionalists seize power without a second thought. Both sides equally think only of the stomach and will amicably split: one is the nearest present, the other is the future. And both will be mistaken in the calculation, because, in reality, a person has more than a stomach; there is also a soul that cannot but speak.

Part Sixteen

This movement among the crowd, due to its chaotic nature, to childish naïveté, to an unimaginable misunderstanding of the actual situation, to many separate, masquerading stupidities, can, of course, leave one only to shrug: a real-life Don Quixote quest.[132] And it as precisely this comparison that occurred to me during my time in prison, when I considered our "propaganda":

Glorious knight of La Mancha
We are brothers in spirit
And your comical name
I'm ready to accept as my own...[133]

When I look back on that crazy time, now standing on the outside, I cannot help but see that in the end, the youth was in the main only guilty of an excessive trust in the tales told in the most prominent literature. Don Quixote went mad at his own expense, but we, as a "proxy". If the people had really been what we imagined them to be, our movement would have been far from ridiculous.

In fact, what did we even know about the participation of the masses in the settled structure of this present, "existing system" we hated so much? The people to us were always portrayed as its *victims*, but not the least its organisers and supporters. Who was it who painted all sorts of "Ponisova Volnitsa"[134] fleeing from "Moscow

---

[132] **(Ed.)** Don Quixote was a novel by the Spanish writer, Miguel de Cervantes (1547-1616), released in two parts in 1605 and 1615. The titular hero, in pursuing knightly heroism, finds his exploits reduced to absurdity in the post-chivalric world.

[133] **(Ed.)** Tikhomirov is here speaking as if addressing the character in Cervantes' book.

[134] **(Tr.)** A nickname for Stenka Razin, difficult to render in English (see p.110).

oppression", various Stenka Razins[135] and Pugachevs[136], "partisan bandits", etc.? Who wrote:

> *And although every year the churches in Russia*
> *Curse this person*
> *The people of the Volga sing songs of him*
> *And remember him with honour...* [137]

and similar nonsense and fiction? Let the readers at least leaf through *The Situation of the Working Class in Russia*, and find what an impossible, untenable position we describe. If even a people "crushed by brute force", etc., have lost the courage needed to "shake off their oppressors", if they bear their load as "dull, gloomy burlaks"[138], and "on the great Russian river" only a "groan is heard", "where the people are, there are groans"; is it not in fact light-minded to conclude that such a downtrodden, suffering people can easily rebel?

Might we assume that our experts in folk life, our teachers, spoke of things they hadn't the least clue about, that which inspired our tearful folk singers and leaped "to the pen from the cards, and to the cards from the pen", only to be waved away?

---

[135] **(Ed.)** Stepan Razin (1630-1671): Russian Cossack rebel leader who launched an insurrection against the nobility of the south, beginning in 1670. It was crushed by the government of Tsar Alexei (1629-1676), and Razin was publicly executed.

[136] **(Ed.)** Yemelyan Pugachev (1742-1775): Russian Cossack rebel leader who launched an insurrection against Empress Catherine II, beginning in 1773. In fomenting the uprising, he posed as the empress' late husband, Peter III (1728-1762), whom she had overthrown in a coup. He was captured and publicly executed.

[137] **(Ed.)** From the poem, *Yest' na Volge utos...* (There is a cliff on the Volga...), by Alexander Navrotsky (1839-1914), a Russian military writer. Despite the poem's popularity among the political left, Navrotsky himself was a conservative.

[138] **(Ed.)** An occupation in Imperial Russia, burlaks hauled barges upstream.

Wake now! There's a greater pleasure:
Call them back. For you are their salvation!
But the sated are to goodness deaf.[139]

We knew nothing of the people, their groans and joys, their actual revolts, their views on freedom and servitude. There used to be some pretty, young lady in a golden pince-nez, in a fashionable dress she had not yet managed to change into peasant rags, who sang in a thin voice:

Freedom, liberty, free will!
To us, swan, will you not fly?..

and this was sincerely deduced, with such stupidity and yet with such conviction, to be a song "discovered" among "peasants" "during a study". Poor, poor "greenhorns"![140] It was not easy for them to pay for broken pots.[141]

And yet, they excite a tragic sentiment only while they are young, while something else could come out of them, while they are a victim of their elders. A dozen years went by, brains froze over completely, sincerity turned into a Chinese stiffness, feeling hardened into sectarian intransigence, eyes closed to everything, and the disfigured generation, in turn, began to mutilate others. They had no place for pity, which their new victims were most worthy of.

---

[139] **(Ed.)** An extract from the poem, *Razmyshleniya u paradnogo podezda* (Reflections at the Grand Entrance), by the Russian poet, Nikolai Nekrasov (1821-1877), a heroic figure to liberal and radical circles for his works which romanticised peasant life.

[140] **(Tr.)** The word in Russian is *zheltorotyye*, literally 'yellow-beaked', that is, an inexperienced and naïve person. Greenhorn would be the English equivalent.

[141] **(Ed.)** A self-explanatory Russian phrase. Tikhomirov is here alluding to the Tchaikovsky Circle's attempts to blend in with the peasants. Students purchased what they believed to be peasant clothes, along with assorted low-quality junk as part of their disguise, often being conned in the process.

Part Seventeen

The young generation of the 70s could attribute no *moral* responsibility for their actions to the people. While the movement claimed to be prompted by conceptions of Russia's social structure in relation to the historical role and present situation of the people, these were exposed as soon as it went among them. From the moment these experiences were had, we took on personal guilt. No matter how short these excursions were, no matter how unimportant the particular activities the circle was engaged in there, there was a lot to learn for anyone who had preserved even the least spark of free consciousness. And everyone possesses this spark. We could not help but see, and truly *saw* much. We knew all too well that among the people we could scold anyone, blame anyone, but it was almost impossible to even hint that the sovereign was to blame. One could *only* mention the sovereign to the most "prepared". Every propagandist learned this in short order. We all knew that the only successful attempt at popular organisation was made by Stefanovich[142] and his comrades, who purported to act on behalf of the Highest Name, directly under his command, and even swore people in his name. The slightest honest reflection on such facts could have revealed to us the true nature of the Russian political system. At every step, we saw Orthodox philosophy among the people, and, with the slightest honest consideration, we could have understood from this not only what the people were, but what the Church which knew how to educate them was. We saw clearly the ideas of the people on property, on power, on the familial principle. We could have, and indeed should have subjected our ideas to revision on the basis of what we observed, but such a revision *was unwanted*. Many of us who lived for extended periods among the people began to experience

---

[142] **(Ed.)** Yakov Stefanovich (1854-1915): Russian revolutionary populist who led a short-lived peasant revolt based on a forged mandate from the tsar in 1877. He served on the Executive Committee of the People's Will in 1881 but was arrested a year later and never returned to the revolutionary life.

a regeneration, and, noticing this, we concluded that being with the people was "bourgeois", "de-revolutionising", and even started to oppose such excursions. Within our circle, people were not only capable of seeing, but did *see* the meaning of elections, collective discussions, etc. Those who were more intelligent soon formed a definite belief that the intelligent are not chosen, and kagal deliberations only confuse questions. We knew that a majority is more stupid than a minority, and in the practices of our own circle we acted in accordance with this fact. Yet, for Russia, for an organism a million times more complex, we continued to demand the supremacy of the people, popular votes, etc.

In general, we could have learned a lot, but in truth we learned nothing. One thing was clear: to be near the people was to be like a fish struggling in ice. Another sentiment, evidently felt, was bitterness because we were being persecuted, because they didn't let us conduct propaganda or prepare popular uprisings (something we loudly declared we were doing), because they threw us in jail or sentenced others to hard labour; and thirdly, of this we are *quite* sure, there was the sentiment that we were the *vanguard* of the inevitable general movement, the revolution, and that therefore we were a force, a tremendous force, not in terms of our present composition, obviously insignificant, but in terms of our position, so to speak. We were not strong in our own right, but as representatives of the inevitably impending revolution.

Part Eighteen

The youth's belief in the revolution in our country was, again, not being created by any conspirators, emigrants or professional revolutionaries. This was what our old "Western" conception imported from France told us, and it was quite logically rooted in our educated class. That the world was progressing with revolutions was, in the era of my education, an *axiom*, a *law*. Whether anybody liked it or not, *she* will come to Russia, if only because she has not yet come; obviously she was to come soon. The more time elapsed without a revolution, the less time we had left to wait. It was so very clear! Of course, possessed of a certain worldview, people were waiting for the "coming" with joy.

> *...The cause is assured*
> *When blood flows beneath it —*

as Nekrasov put it.[143] But a revolution was considered inevitable even by those who did not wish for it in the least. "Oh, immature youth," admonished a police officer during an arrest, "why do you bother with this? Behold, they will erect a monument to you in fifty years: but where will you be then? You'll have disappeared somewhere long ago". Among the people of that time who are now elderly, this belief remains remarkably strong. One very famous writer, a rather definite nationalist and not a liberal at all, just recently told me: "I am most glad that Russia has already *emerged from* her revolution, since I always maintained that we were going through it, and now we can count on a calm development". Notice that this person had to convince himself that the "law" had been fulfilled. Otherwise there could be no calm!

I have already noted above that the popular worldview, leading to a complete contradiction with real life, gives rise to a revolution. But

---

[143] **(Ed.)** This extract is from his poem, *Poet I grazhdanin* (The Poet and the Citizen).

115

the tensions of this world have little to do with it. The world generally does not develop through revolutions. Nor does Russia, considered in a general sense. As for the "progressives", they will never emerge from the "revolution" until their general philosophy changes.

Belief in the imminent revolution reached an extreme degree in the 70s, especially, of course, among the revolutionaries themselves who were comforted to think they did not act in vain. Nechayev even gave precise dates for the revolution. One of them was the year in which temporary liability to landlords was abolished. I remember when I was in prison, the man in the cell next door[144] remarked to me:

"We have gotten to know each other so well, but we've never met in person. Yet, I'll be seeing you…"
"When?"
"When we are free."
"It will be quite a wait!"
"How so? We won't be dead in three years, but in that time, if the court has not released us, *the revolution will*."

This was said quite seriously.

No matter how blind the internal, theoretical faith is, one must however have some external signs. Why did we believe the revolution to be so close? No doubt signs were a necessity. Among the people, however, we saw very little, and this caused us to draw comfort by taking account of the most trifling incidents, the most insignificant clashes of workers with owners, peasants with local police, every muzhik's[145] complaint that "life has gotten hard", everything that is, was, and always will be, which proves nothing beyond the eternal clash of human interests and the infinity of human desire for a better, more convenient lot in life. In a dynamic, vital social equilibrium, we, in our narrow worldview, did not wish to see the overall result, the equilibrium itself, but noted only the oscillations of its individual faces. Observing that there was, as yet,

---

[144] We were knocking, of course. Each letter is indicated by a well-known, short combination of strokes. Having learned, you can talk very quickly, faster than you can, for example, write. We were in such a debate. Some knocks were so second-nature that even the watchman adopted them.
[145] **(Tr.)** A Russian term for peasants.

no revolution, we concluded that the people were being crushed, that they lived in fear and did not dare to rebel. This conclusion, riven with error, filled the appropriate column on the revolutionary sheet. But the real sign of the coming revolution, already quite convincing it seemed, was to be found in the "conscious part of the people", in society, in the intelligentsia.

To trigger a revolution from this jumping-off point, in alliance with "society", was in fact undesirable and unpleasant. But if there was no alternative place to start, what were we to do? We could at least take some comfort from the belief that with the overthrow of the "absolutist" government, the "people who oppress" would be thrown off the "people", who today sit quietly out of fear and tomorrow will take up the revolutionary path.

Part Nineteen

It was undesirable for us to begin "with society", even shameful, for it seemed like a betrayal. Indeed, we were in nowise liberals. We were instead consistent and sincere bearers of the worldview held in common with the liberals, and could therefore be described as extreme democrats, supporters not of mere verbal, but real popular absolutism, political and economic. Everything should belong to the masses. The liberals naturally resisted this. Thus, in helping them to gain power, to introduce a constitution, we felt that we were, so to speak, betraying the people, the people's cause. For this reason, we were unconditionally opposed to a constitution at first. We certainly wanted an economic revolution. It was necessary to have an anarchist mind in order to accommodate the uncertainty of this "economic revolution", but we didn't care in any case.

So, the constitution we did not want, for we feared it, but, meanwhile, we explained all our failures "among the people" by the fact that "the government denies us freedom of action". From this a thought arose which can hardly be called a thought, owing to its absurdity, but which, however, was the first to initiate terror.

I do not have to hand *Land & Freedom*, an underground pamphlet which contained this wisdom, but in essence, the thought went like this: "We do not demand the constitution and freedom in general, for they do not concern us; we have our own cause – socialism. However, we demand that we not be prevented from acting, and if we are interfered with, we will kill members of the administration and the government". In other words: let, if it please you, censorship exist, so long as we are not prevented from publishing underground pamphlets and manifestos; let there be administrative exile, if only the revolutionaries are not expelled; let the police prevent any kind of crime, except the preparation of an uprising...

Obviously, this position was too stupid to be held by anyone for an extended amount of time. And although such things continued to be expressed now and then, the mass of the revolutionary stratum very quickly took the path of a *general* demand for greater liberties. They still talked about "overthrowing the government", "revolutionary seizure of power", "convening a constituent assembly", etc. In their own minds, revolutionaries to a certain extent copied the liberals here, although they remained more radical than them, went further, and, in any case, wished for power not to pass to the liberals, but to the masses, or, "what was the same thing", "to its revolutionary representatives", that is, to themselves.

A thought had emerged from sheer absurdity and hung in the air as fantasies usually do. But unfortunately, this new domain of fantasticality no longer created comic positions, but tragic ones, and led to crime after crime.

Part Twenty

Let us leave aside the moral question. From the point of view of the calculation itself, what did the revolutionaries represent in our time? Did the pure nonsense of a madman, bereft of all consciousness of reality, speak through them?

If I wrote here for the revolutionaries, I would primarily draw their attention to this aspect of things. But for Russia more broadly, it is of greater import not to forget the objective circumstances that produced the illusion succumbed to by vulnerable minds.

So, I will instead ask: was there anything in the mood and behaviour of prominent sections of society which could have given the revolutionaries a reason to contemplate a revolutionary movement in society? Was there anything that justified M. N. Katkov exclaiming, even if in a fit of agitation, that "we are already in a revolution", and Professor N. A. Lyubimov[146] writing his articles of grave warning, *Against the Current*?

The answer is, unfortunately, all too clear. I am not speaking here of the *ideas* that permeated these parts of society, about which there can already be no question, but of their *behaviours*.

Firstly, in these strata of society there was complete confidence in the necessity of a constitution, that the reforms of the late sovereign emperor had their logical conclusion precisely in the restriction of autocracy by the constitution. To this very goal and end the reforms were driven, insofar as was possible. Most of these people, no doubt, not only did not want to achieve the goal through direct violence, but, as I said, had enough common sense to understand the impossibility of violence. However, it is no less certain that they were in a state of irritation and dissatisfaction on the occasion of the prolonged "non-crowning" of the building and were inclined to rejoice at everything

---

[146] **(Ed.)** Nikolai Lyubimov (1830-1897): Russian scientist and ghost-writer for Katkov's *Moskovskie Vedomosti*, where the articles in question appeared. He was a sharp critic of Alexander II's liberal reforms

that would "rush" the government in the interests of "helping society".

All of this was perhaps worse than revolution, but it still did not constitute one. Then, among the youth, the revolutionary movement appeared. How did the liberals see it? Of course, they could not approve of "appealing to the people", but disapproval was far from sharp or convincing. Firstly, the anarchist line of thinking was so powerful that there were quite a few "people of society" who gave succour to this strange movement. Is it really possible to consider such people as Kovalikov and Voynoralsky[147], elected as magistrates, to be "outside society"? During the Trial of the 193, even members of the judiciary, officials and landowners were conflicted. Let's suppose this was only a moderate sympathy, but for the movement it was incredible. Let's suppose that "disapproval" was also expressed by society; but what a disapproval! The youth were reproached for "honourable, magnanimous, etc. *passion*". What a fantastic reproach! When a series of political trials began in 1874, young people themselves saw only sympathy from progressive society. This was based primarily on a sense of *humanity*, but it was impossible to ignore that these same people showed no such humanity in relation to other, non-political criminals. True humanity, which introduces no error, is very rare. There were two or three people who, while providing Christian assistance to suffering people (naturally, we speak here of political prisoners), expressed their disapproval to them, tried to convince them, to prove to them that they were wrong. This was true humanity, not the desire to help *one's own*, but one's enemies, and, moreover, the desire not to soothe and comfort them, but to *save* them, to assist them not only financially, but also spiritually. Yet, such people were a rare exception. For the most part, helping prisoners was an exercise of worship in which they were treated like *martyrs*, and in a spiritual sense, this completely destroyed them. Sometimes, on the part of the "political" in progressive society, there was a clear, unquestionable sympathy for the ideas. The speech by S. Bardina[148] at a trial was a sensation for

---

[147] **(Ed.)** Appears to refer to obscure individuals, S. Kovalikov and P. Voynoralsky, who were members of the Tchaikovsky Circle and later *Black Partition*. See p. v.
[148] **(Ed.)** Sofia Bardina (1853-1883): Russian populist activist who played an important role in attracting women to the revolutionary milieu in the early years. She later committed suicide in Switzerland.

society. The famous Turgenev "reverently" kissed the card of the "martyr". If prisoners, convicts, etc. have heard reproaches to themselves, made entirely of convolutions, then these have only been from the point of view that such energy is fruitlessly wasted which might have been applied to the goal of obtaining political liberties. In general, the behaviour of progressive society was such that only one conclusion could be drawn from it; that while society did not dare believe in such a joyful event as the coming revolution, it very much desired it. Consequently, it was only necessary to heat things, to stir it up; and things will go.[149] Things, it seems, were to go, because according to all that was gleaned from the worldview of "society", the system of government appeared to hang in mid-air, with no solid reason.

The sympathy of "society" for the revolution, freed from its excessive "machismo" and socialism, and aimed at predominantly political goals, was, in the view of the revolutionaries after the era of trials, unquestionable. The revolutionaries had no doubt that they would be accepted with open arms and were only held back by a fear of "betraying the people". However, the people clearly did not anticipate a revolution, and, in the meantime, it was psychologically impossible to further delay persons who were so passionate, so unconditionally faithful to the cause of revolution.

---

[149] **(Ed.)** This is possibly a reference to a well-known phrase of the French economist, Jacques Vincent de Gournay (1712-1759); "Laissez faire et laissez passer, le monde va de lui même" (Let do and let pass, the world goes on by itself).

Part Twenty-one

Much was said about terror, and the revolutionaries themselves searched on numerous occasions for reasons, supposed goals. In my opinion, this "individual revolt" flowed, in the depths of its psychological foundation, not at all from any calculation nor in service to any *goal*. The terrorists did not understand themselves and in this respect would never have sought such understanding. That was the situation. Almost from the cradle, all these people's thoughts and passions were directed towards the revolution. And yet, no revolution appeared, there was nobody to revolt with, not a soul, nobody wanted it. For some time, one could wait, propagandise, agitate, demand, but still, in the end, nobody wanted to revolt. What to do? Wait? Accept? But this would mean confessing to oneself the falsity of one's views, confessing that the existing system is possessed of very deep roots, while the revolution had none or very few. Admitting any of this would necessitate further admissions, and step by step, question by question, the breaking of anyone's revolutionary faith. I remember one neophyte, no longer a boy, who kept pestering the revolutionaries: "Give me the real *doings*, or I will become an informant". I did not understand this strange dilemma then. But indeed, with such an absolute adoration of the revolution, the absence of actual revolutionary *doings* was terrible. After all, theory certainly predicted them; if revolutionary theories and evaluations were true, then *doings*, revolution in fact, *could not fail to come to pass*. Thus, if they were absent, if it was not even possible to conceive of them, then the theory was exposed as so much nonsense and lies; but if it was a lie, then this lie was undoubtedly criminal, so criminal that it needed to be eradicated by all means. And so; "Give me *doings*, or I'll become an informant". I remember they gave him some doings, and in any event, he ended up exiled somewhere.

Without a revolution, the youth of the 70s was threatened with a total collapse of his entire worldview. He could not allow this, for his mind could not become accustomed to doing any actual work and, most importantly, he could not find a *different* faith. There was only one thing left: the individual revolt. If there had been a bit more revolutionary material to work with in Russia, he might have first tried mass barricades or a coup plot. But these turned out to be impossible. Nothing came of them. All that remained was to *act* alone or with a small group of comrades, and therefore to act against *individuals*, secretly, from behind corners... Under this cloak and dagger practice, of course, the most diverse *objectives* were sought: *revenge, disarray, the protection of propaganda*, etc. In the main, it was quite simply the only way to start the revolution, that is, to prove to yourself that it had in fact begun, that all your talk was not just empty phrases.

Part Twenty-two

Such terrible steps had been brewing for a considerable time, and indeed they could not have been taken if the revolutionaries had lacked the time to entirely stupefy their minds and consciences, and even given this, they could not have achieved scale if not for the frivolous and truly criminal behaviour on that part of society, which had supported the illusions haunting the narcotised brains of the terrorists. Yet all these conditions materialised, one after the other, as if by design.

Studying "all sciences" was originally a good thing, acceptable under Lavrov's programme in the self-education circles, and it was good to "read" books as if, like two droplets, we were identical to scientists! But even this entirely bearable encumbrance for the mind of the revolutionary was discarded during the "movement of the people". The denial of the sciences began, and the new formation of the "progressive intelligentsia" managed to reach remarkable ignorance. The revolutionaries of the first period called this new breed "troglodytes". Like fresh lobsters[150], "troglodytes" could say: "Either the sciences confirm the revolution, in which case they are superfluous, or they contradict it, in which case they are harmful".

Yet, this denial of reading, education and books had its own internal logic. What did the revolutionaries have to gain from the science accessible to them, the writings of various liberals? Essentially nothing. In fact, they could only have a cooling effect of inspiring continuous doubt. What reason could there be in wasting time that could have been used "for doings"? There was no love for pure knowledge, nor could this knowledge be established on its own. Not even the practical, the "useful" got a hearing. Education and reading thus received the overwhelming scorn of the youth, something which reflected the influence of the revolutionaries of that time, and the results were sometimes stark. I can recall incredibly

---

[150] *(Tr.)* The meaning is unclear.

talented boys in their first years of schooling, who after two or three years were remarkably dim, as their minds had been immersed into a conceited disaster. Indeed, any science, even the most liberal, would have provided an exercise for the mind, but it was completely abandoned. Revolutionary faith was shackled in an impenetrable armour of habitual reasoning and absent knowledge. Without this, it would have been difficult for the faith to maintain itself, to survive the obvious refutation which cried out from the facts, and to advance to the stage of "terror" without noticing that it was signing its own logical death warrant. Having riveted tightly the springs of comprehension, the only obstacles left for the revolutionary were habits of moral feeling.

It truly is curious how everything just seemed to work out by itself, but with such systematic movement, as if someone had deliberately worked the controls to lead events to their fateful conclusion. Until 1876, there had been no political assassinations (although there were already incitements to them), but in this year a strange debate seemed to arise in revolutionary circles with extraordinary power: *does the end justify the means*? Any outside observer would have concluded that these people were plotting a crime or at least clearing a space for it in their conscience. The revolution half-consciously stumbled upon barriers that could not be overcome by clean methods; so *she searched for ways to excuse* unclean methods. The question was debated with great passion. The dominant circle of 1877-1878, *Land & Freedom*, recognised the rule: "the end justifies the means"; this guiding principle was included in its programme, and after this, no one was allowed into the circle without a solemn profession of this Jesuit principle.

Indeed, from their point of view, the revolutionaries could not but accept it. Their hands at that time were completely shackled by moral concepts. And yet, why not kill, rob, deceive? Why not impose this or that fate upon people by force? Of course, utilitarian morality, the only one they were able to admit, said that murder, violation of another's rights, deceit, etc., were unacceptable because they were harmful to society. As a general rule, this was clear. But what about as applied to *revolutionaries*, the saviours of society, its progressive vanguard, bearers of mankind's conscience? After all, they carried out the revolution, that is, the *greatest good*, the greatest *benefit* to all which corresponded to the greatest degree of *morality*. Therefore, if for such a goal it would be *useful* to kill someone, then the killing would be morally permissible or even necessary. But what if the calculation turned out to be erroneous, and perhaps a murder or a theft was revealed to be useless or inexpedient? This was another matter entirely, and, in any case, the revolutionaries had to rely only on their own considerations because they were more progressive than everyone else, they understood better than anyone, and nobody was in a position to instruct them. If they interpreted something as useful, then in all likelihood it was. Instead, if they heeded the direction of society or the people, they would have been vulnerable to greater errors.

Part Twenty-three

At that time, when the ideas of *terror* were brewing in various ways in the revolutionary milieu, "progressive" society assumed an increasingly oppositional stance. Accustomed to using all the troubles in business as a means of criticism, something which carried hints of "crowning the building" and the need for "assistance", this society also reacted to numerous political trials. This was all the easier because the trials were conducted publicly, noisily, as if the government was deliberately broadcasting them to the people. The sucking up to the defendants, censure of the government and its administration, "destroying the youth"; all this rose to a crescendo. Unfortunately, at that time, everything was developing towards a single end; in the ill-fated Trial of the 193, the case was, in truth, overinflated by the investigation. The *actual* (rather than moral) guilt of the majority of those involved was so insignificant that it was not even worth a trial but required purely administrative penalties. At the same time, the defendants (in the beginning, to my recollection, about six hundred people were involved) did not at all constitute *one* secret society, as the investigation endeavoured to prove. This fundamental error of the investigation meant that the cases dragged on into impossibility. The defendants sat in solitary confinement for four years. This was both cruel and unfair and could not but arouse a real feeling of solidarity, however, more importantly, it served as an excellent pretext for a liberal outcry. Under the influence of all this, the lower administration (I know nothing of what happened in the upper echelons), with which I had to deal, softened remarkably, and ensured I remained entirely guilty. In the place of pre-trial detention (in St. Petersburg), where people gathered to the side of three hundred political defendants, an altogether unthinkable order was established that culminated in the ill-fated clash of the former mayor F.F. Trepov with Bogolyubov, who had been deprived of his "political" rights.

General Trepov, whose form of "solitary confinement" dished out to the political leaders in prison was to incite pure fury (and anyone who remembers such discipline will understand this sentiment), found fault with Bogolyubov for trifles and ordered him to be flogged.[151] I will not justify anyone in this story, since it would be superfluous. The case speaks for itself. It occurred almost on the eve of the release of two hundred defendants for trial, met by rabid crowds. The trial worked out exactly as planned, that is, it was the most scandalous political demonstration, which exposed the weak court as being unable to even finish what it started. The "progressive" public welcomed the "heroes", and then 150 defendants were triumphantly released to the streets of St. Petersburg.

At the entrance to the prison, they met carriages of compassionate sympathisers who offered hospitality to the first "political" prisoners they met. Many doors "in society" were opened before the magic word "liberated". The police behaved towards them with the most helpful courtesy. And yet, in general, the police were so "polite" during this time that it seemed they were all about to retire.

Decidedly, throughout St. Petersburg, many groundsmen[152] kept to themselves, those irreconcilable reactionaries! They alone did not wish to understand the "meaning of events". But the rest (even if their intention was to completely bamboozle the revolutionaries, to finally convince them of the position held by the progressive wing of the general movement), they could not have acted in a more felicitous manner.

The next day, upon the release of the last set of defendants, Vera Zasulich shot General Trepov. After some time, a police agent was killed in Rostov, and in Odessa, armed resistance arose against the police, a real battle. In Petersburg meanwhile, there was no one to resist. Meetings were freely held. Street demonstrations began. In the hospital of St. Nicholas, the "political" prisoner Podlevsky (a Catholic) died.[153] A whole crowd of young people wanted to arrange a solemn funeral for him, not because Podlevsky was noteworthy. Even I only heard his name for the first time then. But it was an excuse for a demonstration. The administration ordered the deceased to be buried without a ruckus, but the crowd broke into the hospital,

---

[151] (*Ed.*) The incident described is that mentioned on p.iii.

[152] (*Tr.*) In Russian, *dvornik*; someone who keeps entranceways clear and communal areas tidy.

[153] (*Ed.*) An obscure revolutionary activist, A. Podlevsky. He was arrested in 1877 for propagandising and quickly fell ill in detention.

captured the coffin and carried it away in triumph. The police blew whistles; gorodovoys[154] and groundsmen came running from all sides. The young female students who carried the coffin were the first to raise their fists, and men rushed to their rescue. A two-minute long fistfight ensued. But from the crowd, more upright people notified the prístav[155]: "Remember, Mr. Prístav, the responsibility for bloodshed will fall on you". And the prístav ordered the gorodovoys to retreat. A crowd carried the coffin throughout the city to the Catholic cemetery... Time passed with adventures such as these, with gatherings seeking programmes of action, before the trial of Vera Zasulich.

She was acquitted to general applause; General Trepov was condemned by "public opinion". "Public opinion" recognised the revolutionaries' right to kill. The end justified the means, and the end was good. It could not have been made clearer. In any case, the induced release of Zasulich from her presumed arrest, newspaper articles on the subject, and finally, the universal harbouring of the "heroine" all served to put a fine point on the justification.

At this moment, Petersburg should, of course, have reminded even F.F. Trepov himself of the familiar paintings of Warsaw on the eve of the uprising.

"Well, I'll tell you", said "one of the smartest revolutionaries" of that time, rubbing his hands, this man who deeply despised "liberals". "I'll tell you resolutely,

By their masters
The beasts thundered:
The cows and the bulls
And yard workers..."[156]

---

[154] **(Ed.)** The lowest rank of urban police in late Imperial Russia.

[155] **(Ed.)** A higher rank of police officer, they had the responsibility of overseeing order and conducting investigations, among other functions.

[156] **(Ed.)** This quote is drawn from an obscure collection of Russian folktales. It can be found in Shen, P. (1898). *Velikoruss v svoikh piesniakh, obriadakh, obychaiakh, vierovanniiakh, skazkakh, legendakh i t.p.* St. Petersburg: Imperatorsko Akademii Nauk, p.300.

And he delved into composing leaflets and invitation cards for the upcoming memorial service for Sidoratsky, who was "killed" during the release of Zasulich.[157]

Who killed him? I have no idea; it seems likely he shot himself. For what purpose? God only knows. Perhaps, indeed, as was said, he knew the crowds would blame the gendarmes.[158] At the time, no serious revolutionary believed in this fairy tale, but in terms of sparking demonstrations, the whole fiasco was absolutely wonderful.

A memorial service was scheduled to last several days. Printed invitations were sent out (even to the police) across the city. Sympathisers were invited to honour the memory of this "victim of despotism" (I don't recall the exact expressions). People even attended the service from Moscow. The extreme revolutionaries of that time wished to seize upon this moment of passion.

The cows and the bulls
And yard workers,

came to bring about a skirmish in the streets. They say that many of them were armed. Indeed, it was easy to assume that the administration would accept the challenge and take the opportunity to purge Petersburg. But things turned out differently. Although troops and masses of police were gathered in nearby spaces, they did not intervene. A memorial service went ahead, as scheduled, in the Vladimir Church. A crowd of people, a thousand people, stood around. Even more curious onlookers crowded on the opposite side of Vladimir Square. At the end of the requiem, everyone poured out into the street. "Gentlemen, look; do not drag students away" ordered dressed up "liberals". But the police didn't touch anyone. A speech began. The speaker, perched on something, very eloquently assailed "despotism", and the prístav peacefully walked around him, in the

---

[157] **(Ed.)** After Zasulich was acquitted on the charge of attempted murder, there was some confusion over her fate, given the unprecedented circumstance. A young *Narodnik* student, Grigory Sidoratsky (1859-1878), opened fire on the police in the middle of a gathering crowd, thinking they had been sent to re-arrest her. It is unclear what happened next. The government claimed he had then shot himself, while his fellow students alleged that the police shot him. This accusation was subsequently repeated in all the major socialist periodicals.
[158] **(Ed.)** Militarised law enforcement.

crowd. It's a picture that can't always be seen in Paris. Then the crowd slowly stretched along the Nevsky[159], and here also they began to "demonstrate", the mounted troops constantly keeping an apparently deliberate distance of two or three hundred steps... Little by little, everyone dispersed without further incident and without any consequences. No arrests occurred either on the spot or afterwards.

---

[159] **(Ed.)** That is, the river Nevsky.

Part Twenty-four

These attempts at demonstrations were repeated from time to time in subsequent years, however, generally speaking, there were too few people "from society" who were ready to turn out. The progressives had enough common sense to understand when and to what extent this could be done. Already in the aforementioned requiem for Sidoratsky, many stayed at home only because they had heard revolutionaries would be carrying revolvers. They understood that if an open riot forced the government to abandon unyielding peacefulness, they would be wiped off the face of the earth by two o'clock or in two days' time. Meanwhile, the administration remained in a markedly softened state for just two months, and then returned to some measures of repression. In some places, arrests and exiles began. Under such conditions, the "progressive part of society" considered that the best course of action was to exploit someone else's revolutionary movement rather than getting personally involved in it. The same witty man that I mentioned was most perturbed and decisively pulled back from all kinds of terror and "politics" in general. "No," he said, "I won't be ripped off by liberals again". This was, of course, not an isolated case. Others, who did not give up their "political liberties," saw again that there was no other action before them apart from terror and the individual revolt. And the terror continued, with the rule established that we were not to act in the open, that we must strike from around corners, with sudden attacks, in the strictest secrecy of a "conspiracy". This approach was unashamedly preached by the pamphlet, *Land & Freedom*. Subsequently, it was raised by foreign pamphlets into an entire ludicrous theory, as if opening for humanity the door to a new form of revolution. I will not linger on this childish nonsense. The crux of the matter until 1879 was that even in terror, in lone wolf killings, there was no substantive strength. All this was carried out across Russia by a dozen or two dozen people who moved from place to place, published proclamations from the non-existent "Executive

Committee", etc. The revolutionaries once again felt their weakness and once again, rather than concluding that their ideas needed to change, instead took things to the next logical step. In the midst of this movement, passionate propaganda emerged calling for forces to unite around terror in unconditional discipline, in blind obedience to the centre (which still needed to be created). Finally (and this we must say), all of these forces, all the forces of "revolution", merged in a single personage who preached the message of *regicide*.

In this *crime suprême*[160], this crime of crimes, the spirit of anarchy found its last word. And with it was uttered, unconsciously, the highest recognition of autocratic power.

This weak, torn shred of "wild meat" that grew in the ulcer of the denationalised layer, this self-styled "revolution", grasped in vain for ways to bring down the *system*. The great country would give them nothing, the "revolution" was *not hers*, had nothing to do with her. The "revolution" could only achieve what could be done by a gang of Chechen abreks[161] seeking to avenge their executed leaders. National Russia, which needed to be destroyed, was unconquerable, unreachable, inaccessible to attack. And so, the "revolution" had to crash its meagre weight down upon the sovereign of Russia, for this was to do *the same thing*.

The autocracy could never have achieved such a striking recognition as was contained in this bloody atrocity!

The only thing that stood between the revolutionaries and madness was learning that even if the sovereign is mortal as a man, he is immortal as an institution, as long as Russia is still Russia, as long as the rays of popular consciousness still refract through this great centre. Attempting to snuff out this luminous point of refraction was something prospectively real; yet as a crime, as a means of political action, such an attempt remained a still greater chimera and nonsense than all the previous activities among the people.

---

[160] **(Ed.)** Fr: *Supreme crime.*

[161] **(Ed.)** A descriptor of inhabitants of the Caucuses that has been used in a variety of different ways since its inception. In this instance, it is used in the derogatory Russian sense to mean a lawless renegade. Groups such as the Chechens were often engaged in low-level guerrilla fighting against the Russian state throughout the Imperial period but were largely unsuccessful in achieving their political aims.

And when the black deed was done, the light shone just as it had before, and the world once again saw that when a "revolution" boils down to atrocities against the representatives of the system, there is no revolution, nor can there be one.

Part Twenty-five

The terrorist movement was a conclusion, internally quite logical, but as I have already said, one which was reached only by *the revolutionaries themselves*. Society, even its most progressive members, did not embrace it. The most consistent liberal émigré, Drahomanov,[162] unconstrained by any censorship, immediately reacted to terrorism very unsympathetically. I consider it to be quite convincing to refer to this, because Drahomanov is in no way different from our other constitutionalists, except for his superior experience and political education. But he spoke "freely"; abroad, without censorship, without fear.

Progressive society stood apart from the terrorists. However, I do not wish to exaggerate the distance between the two.

Firstly, I repeat: terrorism would be completely unthinkable if the main substance of the Russian "progressive" worldview wasn't anarchist in nature. This worldview completely rocked the foundations of *morality*; it deprived a person of any solid guidance in determining what he can allow and what he cannot. Drahomonov could arbitrarily blame the terrorists for the theory of "exceptional morality", but he had no way of proving to them that they were wrong, because in the end, in turning away from their methods, he could only be led by instinct. The general "ideals of progress", as defined by the liberals, led (and the least we might say here is that they were sincerely ignorant of this) to the goals of the revolutionaries.

The elimination of the obstacles that lay in the way of these ideals was fatally seen as a moral affair. The emigrant Lavrov, whose moral concepts mirror the opinions of a very significant part of

---

[162] **(Ed.)** Mikhail Drahomanov (1841-1895): Russian political theorist and partisan of *ethical socialism*, who influenced the development of liberalism and separatism in the Ukraine, albeit from abroad.

"progressive society", [163] *was also at first against terror, but in the end he was forced to admit that his "young friends" were more logical than him, and he himself had to craft a syllogism, justifying them.*

"The Russian progressive", he wrote in 1885, "cannot hesitate in choosing a path [...] This struggle is not yet the yearned-for kingdom of moral principles, but an inevitable prerequisite for the triumph of that kingdom [...] Not a single step on this ladder (that is, the struggle) can be skipped [...] The social revolution promises to be bloody and cruel, but its goal is a moral goal and must be achieved". In this case, to hesitate means "to be in danger of acting immorally, of hindering the triumph of the kingdom of moral principles" (*Bulletin of 'The People's Will'*, No. 4, p.83).

The indirect connection between terrorism and the ideas of a certain part of "society" could not but be reflected in the purely practical consequences of that part's behaviour. This abominable fact, shameful in light of any moral sense and for the political significance of society, is nonetheless a fact that cannot and should not be forgotten. Otherwise, we'll never learn. That's how facts work.

In the present moment so filled with crimes positively unprecedented in history, unprecedented because they were not even committed in the course of a *real* revolution, but as self-proclaimed crimes, crimes expressing a positively unprecedented attempt to usurp, crimes in comparison with which the frenzy of the French Revolution's terrorists looks like the rule of law; at such a moment, our Russian society contains at least some individuals who directly assist killers. I will not recite the political trials that established this fact. Let me remind you of the fact that the monthly budget of the "Executive Committee", for several years, fluctuated at around 5,000 roubles a month. Of course, it was not students who gave "to the cause" these 60,000 roubles a year! It might even be more shameful that there were people who shied away from direct help, but who treated the network of political killers as just a *warring faction* and allowed themselves to remain "neutral". Finally, others chose this moment for constitutional agitation. The revolutionaries acted like tigers; these gentlemen chose the role of jackals. The revolutionaries,

---

[163] I repeat that Lavrov set forth his doctrine of morality in legal, uncensored literature, even gaining the title of, "our respectable," "our famous," etc.

like bandits, pulled a knife; these gentlemen tried to then use that same knife to enforce the conditions for their assistance. Morally, this lowland is completely incomprehensible, and, on the one hand, it could arouse only the contempt of the revolutionaries, while on the other, it completely corrupted them. If the terrorist ever had any doubts as he waited in his sap or ambush, he only had to remember the "addresses" or other supportive articles found in the magazines of "loyal subjects" in order to shake off all reproaches, all reason, and hold his head up high.

"The will of the Almighty has been accomplished", we read in the *Order* in March 1881, "now we can only *reconcile* ourselves to the indestructible will of Providence and, *without entering into a futile struggle with it*, devote care to lay a solid foundation for the future [...] Sire, ask your land in the person of your beloved people". The *Country* (Issue 27) speaks of "responsibility for everything that is done in Russia, economic errors, reactionary measures, exile in Eastern Siberia", accuses the "leaders of reaction" and concludes:

"It is necessary that the main features of internal political measures be inspired by representatives of the Russian land. And let the personality of the Russian tsar henceforth serve *only as a symbol* of our national unity", etc. The *Voice* (Issue 36) says that from all that has happened "it has become clear that there is a need for a public organisation to serve with the government" and that it is now necessary to initiate "further reforms, calling on social forces for assistance".[164]

Even the revolutionary chronicle, considering all these features of decomposition beneficial for the revolution, could not fail to notice that "the zemstvo, usually so silent, spoke *at the very moment when even the open enemies of the sovereign found it possible to state their demands only with all kinds of reservations* and reference to the conditions of the moment which would no longer allow them to indulge in a *sense of natural delicacy*" (*Bulletin of People's Will*. T. I. P. 37).

I will not quote here these "zemstvo" statements, which could fill several pages. And although the zemstvo, in the sense of not only its people, but even in the sense of its statements and rulings, was

---

[164] **(Ed.)** The papers mentioned here were all popular liberal publications of the time.

primarily guilty of stupidity and lack of control, thanks to which political charlatans could palm off their "addresses" to the people who had no idea what they were doing, nevertheless this zemstvo should not forget what kinds of people it enabled. Had it been more aware, it could have easily spotted the handful of people trying to fool it, under the guise of some kind of "constitution", and what a false, absurd fiction "public opinion" is, understood in the sense of the outcry of the moment.

The behaviour of that handful of liberal politicians who took upon themselves the mantle of "expressing the views of progressive society", this behaviour, which I characterise by no means using the most cutting instances now rushing into my memory, this behaviour could only completely smother the moral and political consciousness of the revolutionaries. The terrorist heard the scolding accusation of being "seditious", "criminal", etc. But from the behaviour of "progressive representatives of society", he concluded that these were just empty words. Were his actions really immoral when placed alongside this behaviour? Was he truly a usurper in comparison with them? He was instead convinced that he was only a man on the frontlines, and nothing more, that he was doing only what others were thinking about. Terror would never have grown to such proportions, would never have reached its blind fanaticism, if there was no objective justification for its delusion in the form of the behaviour of a certain part of society.

If society understood this, it would certainly not allow its "progressives" their more than ambiguous role; it would not read the newspaper, the leading articles of which remain indistinguishable from the speeches of revolutionary pamphlets; it would not allow dubious persons into public institutions; it would not allow the confusion of legal and illegal, honest and dishonest; it would not tolerate all this muddy water and would force *friends* and *foes* to divide into two clear, discernible camps. And such is its duty, as much as its interest. If this was done, the revolutionaries themselves would see what they are, see the unheard-of dimensions of their usurpation, comprehend its impossibility, and retreat.

But none of this has occurred, thanks precisely to the progressive, extreme wing of the liberals. On the contrary, as much fog was let in as circumstances allowed. And if, in the end, Russia did figure it all out, it would do so not only in spite of, but in active opposition to those who dare to call themselves the "intelligentsia", "the conscious part of the country", etc., aided in this opposition by the most magnificent personages. Those who really have sought to disperse the fog, like M.N. Katkov and I.S. Aksakov, are of course vilified by this "conscious part" as reactionaries.

Part Twenty-six

The "advanced", "progressive" and so on and so forth, worldview has weighed upon everything during these past years. It showed not only its ends in its revolutionaries, but also in the entire balance of moderate and extreme forces. These extremes are logical, as everywhere, and fanatic, like nowhere else. Even as an insignificant impotence, they do not stop at any violent action, nor at any usurpation, nor at any crime. Do not expect any concessions from them either to common sense, or to human feeling, or history. This is the *Russian* revolution, a movement based neither in politics, nor economics, nor any needs, even those faked or inflated by improvements in living standards. This is indignation against real life in the name of an *absolute ideal*. This hunger is insatiable, because it desires what is essentially impossible, and has desired it since it lost God. Having returned to God, such a person can become an ascetic, but until then, he is possessed. He is a revolutionary of revolutionaries. He can't sit still, because if his ideal is impossible, then there is nothing in the world worth living for. He would rather exterminate all "evil", that is, the entire world, everything that exposes his chimera, than succumb.

There is no concession in matters of faith, and if the devil himself wanted to trap a man, he would not be able to conceive of a better trick than directing faith into this hopeless, barren waste, where, apparently with pure intentions, a person inevitably ends up a criminal, devoid of moral feeling itself.

And next to this passionate fanatic, blind and deaf to everything except his *idée fixe*[165]; there is a bankrupt liberal society, the weakest mentally in all of Europe, the most prone to losing its most energetic people to the revolution, lit up itself with the same fever, itself not having durable foundations for either morality or reason. Its influence is enormous when it comes to cultivating revolutionaries, but

---

[165] **(*Ed.*)** Fr: *Obsession*.

insignificant when they need to be restrained. Here, the former teachers themselves are dragged by the students.

If our liberals could understand even for a moment what this situation promises them, especially hearing the ease with which their students pronounce the word "terror", they would be horrified. In the end, danger, struggle, death are nothing to fear when you will commit your very bones to an ideal. But to be killed by your ideal, for Rouget de Lisle[166] to hear his own "Marseillaise", screamed by those who seek to drag him to the guillotine, that is fearful. Only liberals have no desire to understand this, just as the revolutionaries have no desire to understand their crime: because it would leave them without a worldview, without a philosophy, without a faith. Supposing some outlook is fearful or absurd, what can one do? Can he abandon everything; from "reason" through to "human dignity", "freedom", "individual rights" etc.? Are these very fundamentals wrong? Or can he return to the "domostroy"[167] (of course, assuming he is aware of it)? No, unthinkable. It's better to try to avoid *"reductio ad absurdum"*.[168] Ah, how difficult it is when they set out precisely from the absurd!

The liberal only dreams, so he can avoid thinking things through to their end. The revolutionary seeks all salvation by taking things to their logical conclusion. But the fate of both is the same: both are condemned to be dashed against the rocks of reality, from where only the reaction can rescue them. And then, having rested up, having forgotten as much of the experience as possible, they will return to their old story, and to console themselves they will perceive events as if they constitute a "law"; that the world supposedly progresses through "actions" and "reactions". So, the lamp burns quietly, without any "actions" and "reactions" while there is oil, but when the

---

[166] **(Ed.)** Claude Rouget de Lisle (1760-1836): French military poet and composer who authored the country's national anthem, *Le Marseillaise*, in 1792. Despite this, his royalist sympathies landed him in prison under the revolutionary government and he narrowly escaped execution.

[167] **(Ed.)** A set of guidelines for the domestic life of Russians, written anonymously in the 16th century. It later acquired a pejorative connotation among the Russian left for its authoritarian bent.

[168] **(Ed.)** Lat: *the establishment of a claim by showing that the opposite scenario would lead to absurdity or contradiction.*

time is up, the flickering begins; "actions" and "reactions". Formula of death agony! And this is the "law of life", the "law of progress"!

No, such is not the law of life, but it's useless to discuss this until people are convinced that their modern "progressive" ideal is false, impracticable from beginning to end, that it delivers nothing of what is expected from it and which is paid for with so many victims.

ALSO AVAILABLE FROM TAXIARCH PRESS

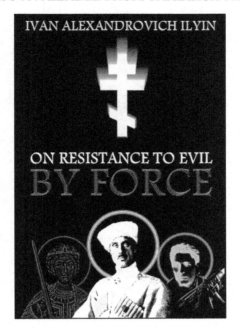

Written in 1925, *On Resistance to Evil by Force* is one of the most important tracts composed by white émigré philosopher Ivan Alexandrovich Ilyin. Responding to the pacifist pretentions of Count Leo Tolstoy, Ilyin mounts a tenacious defence of the Orthodox tradition of physical opposition to evil. As he explains, in the face of evil which can be contained by no other means, a forceful response is not only permissible, but becomes a knightly duty. Further, heroic courage consists not only in recognising this duty, but in bearing its heavy moral burden without fear.

In his own time, Ilyin penned this guide for the exiled Russian White Army in its continued resistance against the godless Bolsheviks, yet while the world has developed since the civil war which he lived through, Christians everywhere can still find great relevance in his words, for the same evil continues its designs through other means and under other names.

Translated here into English for the first time, *On Resistance to Evil by Force* is destined to become a classic of Christian ethics.

OTHMAR SPANN

The True State

Lectures on the Demolition & Reconstruction of Society

Published in 1921, *The True State* (Der Wahre Staat) is the magnum opus of distinguished Austrian economist and sociologist, Othmar Spann (1878-1950). Following the First World War, Spann was the most sought-after lecturer at the University of Vienna, counting such future personalities as Hayek, Morgenstern and Voegelin among his students. Eschewing an entirely academic existence, he also endeavoured to reshape post-war society.

In *The True State*, Spann lays out his grand vision both in economic and sociological terms, seamlessly blending German Idealism with Catholic social values, a critique of Marxist theory and individualist philosophy. His brilliance as an orator and his reimagining of an estates-based culture, inegalitarian but socially conscious, gained him an army of acolytes, but also powerful adversaries in the turbulent interwar period.

As one of the last century's most devastating critics of the contemporary economic and social order, Spann has largely been buried by the academic establishment of today, but his timeless ideas will still hold an appeal for those dissatisfied with modern society. Translated here into English for the first time, and with an extensive introduction from Ellery Edwards detailing the political activities of Spann and his followers, the core message of *The True State* has perhaps never been more relevant.

Described by some as the 'Russian Nietzsche', Konstantin Leontiev (1831-1891) was one of the most enigmatic Russian philosophers of the 19th century. A staunch defender of tsarist autocracy, he offered a radical critique of modern egalitarian culture and politics, particularly from an aesthetic point of view. *Byzantinism & Slavdom* examines the legacy of Byzantium and its vital relevance for understanding Russia and forging its future, distinct from the prevailing ethos of Europe which Leontiev diagnosed as undergoing a civilisational death.

What distinguished Leontiev's aristocratic outlook from that of Nietzsche was his enduring loyalty to the Orthodox Christian faith, without which he predicted Russia would perish. Beyond its remarkable prophecies of WWI and the European Union, this 1875 work is a critical text in the Russian philosophy of history.

Translated into English for the first time and introduced with commentary from K. Benois, *Byzantinism & Slavdom* is essential reading for anyone who truly wishes to grasp the rise and decline of civilisations, driven by titanic laws of natural development, and what these mean for Russia.

Made in the USA
Las Vegas, NV
06 June 2023

73032189R00105